Library of
Davidson College

LYRICS FROM SHELTERS

Modern Chinese Poetry 1930–1950

Selections, Translations, and Introduction by
WAI-LIM YIP

GARLAND PUBLISHING, INC.
NEW YORK & LONDON 1992

Copyright © 1992 by Wai-lim Yip
All Rights Reserved

Library of Congress Cataloging-in-Publication Data

Lyrics from shelters: modern Chinese poetry, 1930-1950/ selections, translations, and introduction by Wai-lim Yip.
   p. cm. — (World literature in translation ; 26)
   ISBN 0-8240-0045-5
   1. Chinese poetry—20th cent.—Translation into English
   I. Yip, Wai-lim. II. Series
PL2658.E3L97   1992
895.1'15108—dc20   92-25625

Printed on acid-free, 250-year-life paper
Manufactured in the United States of America

For Tzu-mei
June
David
& Jonas

Preface

It is not solely because I have lived with, learned from, and taught the poems in this anthology for over thirty-five years, or because the poets presented here were my models during my early years of apprenticeship as a poet, that I have decided to translate them. The significance of this project should be clear to anyone aware of modern Chinese literary history and the fact that because of the unfortunate political changes of the late 1940s, the works of many of the poets in this book, which represent the best tensional dialogues emerging from the confrontation between native sensibility and intruding alien ideologies, had been buried by the events of the time. Only a few insignificant poems by the poets of the 1930s are included in the literary histories and critical notices written *after 1949* and almost none of the creative and critical efforts by the poets of the 1940s have been given a chance to voice themselves. Their commitment to an original style and to the refinement of language as an art made it impossible for historians and critics in Communist China to mention their names without being severely criticized by the Party. Nor were these poets given due recognition in Taiwan during the first thirty years of the Nationalist rule, in part, because their works were unavailable under the general blockage of the flow of Mainland China books to the island. Indeed, until recently, most of them were unknown to the younger generation of both China and Taiwan. Only with the reissuance of some of the poets' individual collections and the publication of the *Nine Leaves Anthology* in the post-Mao Era has the younger generation begun to rediscover and relearn this forgotten legacy.

It must be noted that by now few readers can view these works with an impartial historical sense, having been influenced far too long by the Party-ordained historical narratives, narratives that have, unfortunately, also affected Western scholars and students of modern

Chinese literature. It is my hope that this anthology will help to stimulate others to vindicate these poets and readjust Western readers' perception of this important legacy. Also, in order to help Western readers to avoid the pitfall of reading and judging these works merely against stylistic markers of Western literature—a practice that has inadvertently appropriated the Other into the discourse of the West, and, in doing so, has often ended up distorting it—I have written two introductory essays to serve as entrances into this legacy. A third essay by Dr. Ping-kwan Leung of the University of Hong Kong is included at the end to fill out historical details that my larger theoretical framework cannot accommodate.

In the preparation of this anthology, several poets and friends have assisted in various ways and to them I would like to acknowledge my debts: to Yuan Kejia, Hang Yuehe, Tang Shi and Zheng Min for providing me with biographical details of themselves and fellow-poets; to Bian Zhilin and Xin Di for hours of fruitful conversations during my 1981 and 1982 visits to China; to Paul Pickowiz, Chairman of the Chinese Program in the University of California, San Diego, for providing secretarial assistance; to Susan Brennecke for typing all the translations, and last but not the least, to my wife, Tzu-mei, for years of continual support that has made this and other writing projects a constant pleasure.

Del Mar, Ca.
1990.

Contents

Introductory Essays

   I. Modernism in a Cross-Cultural Context   1
   II. Language Strategies and Historical Relevance in the
       Poetry of 1930–1950   15
   III. Literary Modernity in Chinese Poetry, by Leung Ping-Kwan   43

The Poetry

Feng Zhi	69
Dai Wangshu	75
Ai Qing	83
Bian Zhilin	99
He Qifang	109
Cao Boahua	115
Zhang Kejia	119
Xin Di	123
Wu Xinghua	131
Mu Dan	137
Du Yunxie	147
Zheng Min	155
Chen Jingrong	165
Hang Yuehe	173
Tang Qi	181
Tang Shi	191
Yuan Kejia	197
Lu Yuan	201
About the Poets	207
About the Editor	217

Introductory Essays

I. *Modernism in a Cross-Cultural Context*

Modernism considered as a movement or style in art and literature first began as a Euro-American phenomenon. How are we to treat the various modernisms developed later in non-Western cultures? One prevalent approach is to evoke markers of Western modernism. But immediately a host of questions arise: can we, or should we, talk about modernism in non-Western countries with the same terms we use for Euro-American modernism? The evocation of Western markers has at least two implications: one is that all non-Western modernisms are simply derivative versions of the West. Are they simply so? Another is that these markers are true-to-type signatures of a style, and that whenever these markers appear in a given text, we can declare the work as modernist. Is this necessarily so? Since there are so many "historical narratives" about the rise of modernism in the West and each narrative identifies a different set of markers, some may be diametrically opposed. Which historical narrative are we to follow? Privileging one necessarily suppresses the others, creating only a seeming validity. Is there a master narrative that can accommodate all different sets of markers? As we can see, none of the above questions can be answered easily, and I do not intend or claim to answer them in full here. But, these questions will at least lead us out of the imprisonment critics have willfully set for themselves. Anyone considering them will probably agree that we cannot use a simple yes or no to answer any of them without considerable qualifications.

Clearly, the first thing that needs to be done is to examine metacritically the pitfalls of imposing Western markers upon works of other cultures. Because I have written extensively upon this subject,[1] I am not going to repeat myself here, but instead, let me say this: even in works that bear a clear stamp of influence from the West, we cannot assume that what is true of the source-model must also be true of its transplanted product. There are always native elements that will condition the process of transplantation. We must further ask these questions: under what cultural climate or political and social conditions did the Oriental poets—we will use modern Chinese poets as our example—discover perspectives and strategies compatible with those of the Western modernists? Or, to slightly modify the question, what did they get from Western modernism that filled their need to express the specific cultural and psychological conditions in which they found themselves? To answer this first set of questions is to identify the unique *situatedness*—to borrow a Sartrean term promoted by Fredric Jameson—of both the Western and the Chinese cultural phenomena so as to map out the exact ways in which the two trajectories converged and diverged, and for what historical exigencies. The unfolding of this *situatedness* will allow us to identify other significant issues. We must now ask: what kind of historical necessity prompted the Chinese writers to reject traditional canons and accept a certain alien ideology? In the course of the acceptance, what native ideological aesthetic models were resorted to (albeit unconsciously) for support and justification? What kind of modification was being made in the midst of ideological tensions in order to localize a given alien model for native acceptance? What intellectual and aesthetic obsessions or memories in the native world view, including a theory of history and mental habits (again, albeit open denunciation of them) had conditioned their rejection of certain dimensions of an imported theory or strategy?

Let us now go back to the question of markers. The most frequently used markers (highlighted, but not exhaustive here) are: on the content side, alienation, reification, fragmentation, dehumanization, solipsist subjectivity, etc; and on the formalistic side, leap of logic (paratactic or disruptive syntax), multilinearity, synchronic structure and spatial co-extension, indeterminacy, language revolution, including privileging the word ("Style is absolute"; "the Word is the World"; "language calling attention to itself") and the aesthetic ("Beauty is Religion"), priority of the image (object over idea; the concrete over the abstract; anti-discursiveness), obscurity, dream logic etc. In most of the studies of Western modernism, we will find various attempts to link the formalistic markers to those of the content. Indeed, their linkage has been convincingly argued as culture-specific. For example, it has been advocated, under various guises, that the emergence of these markers is a reflection of, as well as a reaction to, the positivistic reduction of the lifeworld brought about by radical industrialization and urbanization that characterize monopolized capitalism. With exchange value as the dominating form of ossification resulting from accelerated fragmentation, man finds himself in a double jeopardy facing the existence of his natural self and the authenticity of his language. Writing now becomes an odyssey through the senses, the only mechanism as it were, with which he can reclaim his *felt* existence or resurrect that which culture, now an industry aided by new myths of technocracy and commercialism, has completely shattered. Writing now becomes an odyssey through language with full attention to it as it is, because language, now stripped of all the holistic correspondences it once had, must reclaim itself, albeit in a *tour-de-force* manner, by freeing itself from its instrumental characteristics.

But if indeed these markers are culture-specific, can these same markers emerge from a historicity radically different from that of the West, such as is the case in modern China? Take the intriguing phenomenon of cultural and aesthetic interchange that occurred in the 1910s. In matters of aesthetic strategies, the West and China practically changed roles: one appropriated what the other had abandoned, so to speak.

In my *Ezra Pound's Cathay* and "Classical Chinese and Modern Anglo-American Poetry: Convergence of Languages and Poetics" I listed some ten distinctive stylistic features that can be seen as characterizing both poetries, among them, (1) nonanalytical and nondiscursive ideas giving rise to direct and concrete acting-out of things; (2) temporization of space and spatialization of time leading to co-extension of visual events, spatial tensions, pictorial and sculptural qualities; (3) syntactical flexibility and indeterminacy yielding a multiple suggestiveness; (4) non-linear, non-causal or multilinear and synchronic progression; (5) decrease or disruption of connectives to promote strong visuality, concreteness and independence of objects; (6) removal of the speaker (in different degrees and complexities) so as to allow the reader-viewer to participate in completing the aesthetic experience; (7) viewing things as they are; (8) the use of montage (montage being a concept inherited from the Chinese character, see Eisenstein) to achieve a beauty consisting of overlays; (9) (with fewer attempts in the West) diffusion of self into the Undifferentiated Whole, into the million changes of things.[2]

Interestingly, in the early part of the modern period in China, the Chinese poets, instead of continuing from these important aesthetic dimensions, began by moving away from them; they sought more syntactical structures, promoted discursiveness, and adopted rigidified grammar and punctuation which the Western modernists attempted to diffuse, if not exactly destroy.

These paradoxes and ambiguities are enigmatically complex. They force us to retrace the trajectories through which the two movements had departed from their respective hermeneutical systems of quite different aesthetic and cultural orientations. In tracing these two etiologies, we must also try to understand how each of these hermeneutical movements, in a mystifying way, had become a form of tyranny over consciousness and expression, which writers and intellectuals have been consciously and unconsciously attempting to overcome, and against which they have tried to erect and resurrect various forms of counter discourses and new *raisons d'etre*. It must be noted here, too, that it was in part the awareness of these paradoxes and ambiguities that had made it possible for Chinese poets of the 1940s (in mainland China) and the 1960s (in Taiwan) to modify Western modernist techniques with classical Chinese poetics into a new synthesis to form a larger context of modernism in China.

It is now clear that this larger context cannot be discussed from isolating markers of Western modernism as such. It is also clear that the vulgar Marxist use of base and superstructure, such as the statement that capitalist society breeds decadent modernist art, is totally off the mark. But *even* in very sophisticated neo-Marxist attempts, including Fredric Jameson's marvellous critical apparatuses, new modifications must be made. While we can endorse almost everything Fredric Jameson has to say, often with tantalizing comprehensiveness and persuasion, about the dialectical relationship between political and economical conditions and literary and artistic movements and forms, his explanatory frameworks attributing the rise of realism, modernism, and postmodernism in the West respectively to market capitalism, high capitalism, and multinational trade become problematic when applied to the situation in China and other Oriental countries. The rise of modernist aspects in China, some of which emerged as early as the 1920s, definitely did not evolve from the exact same conditions, and indeed, they appeared on the literary scene even *in the absence of them.* We must now try to revise and expand these frameworks in such a way that we can better accommodate both cultural conditions. Here, we are aptly reminded by suggestions of Althusser, V.N. Voloshinov and in some of Jameson's recent writings. Althusser proposes that within a certain historical-economical time frame, more than one factor can give rise to formalistic and stylistic changes—such as when one style exhausts itself, it immediately calls for a change without necessarily being propelled by an economic force.[3] The relationship between socio-political and economical conditions and aesthetic matters can yet be seen in another way. According to V.N. Voloshinov, while all signs are social and ideological since they were invented for communication between two or more persons, they are not class-restricted. The so-called language (diction, style, etc.) of one class is constantly invaded by the language of other classes, because in the arena of real world events, this interplay of various language strategies in synthetic overlays is inevitable.[4]

Any movement in a cross-cultural context necessarily involves an examination of the ground upon which cross-cultural activities—confrontation, negotiation, convergences, divergences and eventual modifications—first take root. This ground of intellectual condition, the situatedness of cultural change and growth, can never be fully recovered if approaches are made hegemonically only from one single cultural perspective without learning to see both ways at once. Fredric Jameson, in a recent reading of Gadamer, talks realistically about interpretation in this instructive manner :

> Each hermeneutical confrontation, between an interpreter and a "text," between an interpreter of one culture and the text of another culture, always mobilizes, at each pole of the interpretive encounter, a whole deployment of prejudice and ideology: one in terms of which the text, as an act, is to be understood, the other which motivates the interpreter in his attempt to appropriate this alien act. Such false problems as that of the "suspension of

disbelief" imply that historical distance of this kind . . . is the fundamental barrier to understanding and needs in one way or another to be lifted, abolished or "suspended" in order for any adequate "historical" understanding or reading to take place . . . Not only is this ideal of some abolition of the content of prejudices of either or both sides of the hermeneutic encounter impossible, but such a suppression would in any case be undesirable, since what is wanted is very precisely just this encounter between the ideological fields of text and interpreter. "Fusion" is not to be understood as the abolition of difference, as the "formation of one horizon" . . . but a preservation of tension, a coexistence within radical difference, a relationship by way of radical difference.[5]

In the case of modern China, this is a period in which the battle and negotiation between the Chinese and Western cultural models have been most intriguingly complex, in which the confrontation between them has deeply disturbed the native sensibility, and its sense of order and value. In order to maintain their *raison d'etre,* the native intellectuals, playing the role of the oppressed, have been struggling either to seek parallels in the imported models or to militantly assert the primacy of their indigenous mental horizon. In the process of this interaction with interpenetrating planes and surfaces of the past and the present, native and alien cultures, modern Chinese literature emerges as an example of cross-fertilization that reveals both the problematics and the strategies central to the studies of the interworkings of cultures.

Presently, we will examine a series of issues such as the iconoclastic distrust and blast of traditional political-aesthetic frameworks, the rethinking of language's ability and inability to authenticate experience, the invention and re-invention of language, language calling attention to itself, the effect of science on consciousness and on expressive strategies, the role of the artist in society, the riddle of the self, etc. But before we wade through these complex issues, we must confront still another larger metacritical question, namely, which of the many "historical narratives" about modernism are we to follow and in what way or ways can they become critically illuminative for the situation in China.

Naturally, we cannot cover all the "histories" of modernism. For our purpose, let us dwell upon three interrelated narratives. Most discussions of modernism try to locate its emergence in the late nineteenth century when consciousness was a great stake in the acceleration of industrialization and the specialization of knowledge, etc. But another view, promoted by the Frankfurt school including Habermas' modification, holds that the aesthetic modernism emerging from the nineteenth century cannot be fully understood without the larger context of the making of the modern. This view sees the problematics of modern consciousness as collateral with the cultural formations of humanism that prevailed since the eighteenth century, if not the Renaissance. Specifically, it was the challenge of the hermeneutical framework underlying the once unified world view and consciousness which dominated Medieval and Renaissance Europe, that ushered in the extremely complex and ambiguous role of the New Philosophy. It was ambivalent because this history can be written as the dawn of humanism since that challenge brought in with it the challenge of the power structure invested in the Church and in the Prince. In one significant sense, this was the beginning of a process of liberating men from arbitrarily "constituted," but at root suppressive prisons of "beliefs"—the beginning of the demythologization of the so-called "truths." And yet the writing of this history is not without its biases. With the prioritization of the rational, emphasizing the kind of verifiability natural sciences had offered, a host of other so-called illogical, irrational, but in reality, alternative forms of consciousness were exiled. Indeed, any other form of thinking deviating from this new emphasis had to be justified. This we see in Kant, for example, who had to ask, with even more persistence than ever, this question: how is reliable and accountable knowledge constituted? To this question, he posited, for most social sciences to follow, a transcendent judge-like reason comparable to that used in natural sciences. With this, he attempted to diffuse the hermeneutical and interpretive crisis of the West. The ambivalent attitude artists and poets of subsequent centuries held toward science can also be understood in this light.

Now the crisis of consciousness has emerged in very disturbing forms. While the West must be thankful to Copernicus and Galileo for breaking the Medieval mythico-political cosmological framework, which led to the birth of the Enlightenment, the enlightened man was, paradoxically, also left in a new wilderness. Before the break, the world was cohesive, all three levels, the macrocosmic, the earth, the microcosmic, rolled into one, with a network of interpretive markers, arbitrarily constituted and antinatural though they were, that were unified and understood throughout Europe. After the break, the truly universal cohesive framework is yet to be found. We see a lot of nostalgia for the so-called unified sensibility in Pound, Eliot and T.E. Hulme, for example. In a sense, all the attempts from Kant on, including the Romantics, the Symbolists, the Modernists, the Phenomenologists, the Existentialists, the Imagists, etc., can be considered as ways of finding alternative explanatory systems, either working from within or borrowing from outside, such as the Oriental, the African and other cultures, to replace this lost world. The break also forced Kant and others to frame new ways of justifying the apparently diverse and unrelated modes of intellectual activities which were at once interdefining and interweaving. In Max Weber's words, at least three separate autonomous realms exist, namely, the cognitive-instrumental, the moral-practical, and the aesthetic-expressive. The separation between truth and beauty as part of this process both disturbed and supported Baudelaire and others, and gave rise to the subsequent alternative claims of "the Word is the World," "Style is absolute," "Beauty is Religion," and "A poem has an autonomous existence" ("A poem does not mean / but be.")

The break continued to give rise to various "gods and ghosts." Indeed, the accelerated specialization, fragmentation, compartmentalization and reification in the work of science-propelled industrialization has continued to break knowledge into numerous self-referential worlds—so much so that many scholars (e.g., Lyotard) are tempted to see the increasingly mutually-exclusive disciplines as new markers of the postmodernist period.[6]   Another consequence of this compartmentalization of knowledge was that the poet was left with no role to play. He was no longer asked to speak for nature, or to account for God's scheme of things. Suddenly, the poet had no altar in society. He had to isolate himself from the masses and from the market which was dominated by the principle of exchange value, so as to preserve the higher value his art once had, but at the same time, willy-nilly, he had to submit himself to their domination.

1. Modernism in a Cross-Cultural Context

It is against this etiology that many scholars see modernism either as a counter-discourse to monopoly capitalism and culture industry (such as the views of Adorno and Horkheimer) or as an avant-garde political program to frontally attack bourgeois institutions (such as the views of Benjamin and Brecht) and see self-proclaimed purity, ambiguous and multiple signification as well as iconoclastic gesture as part of an expressive necessity to recover the deeper meanings of humanity and social ambience.

The ambivalent role of language can also be explained now. On the one hand, to resist the one-dimensional use of language under the influence of positivistic instrumental impulse, poets called for the precision of vagueness (multi-linearity, indeterminancy) by breaking syntax and chronology to achieve a radiating cluster of signifiers. On the other hand, to denounce the falsifying rhetoric of nineteenth-century writing, they called for the use of natural speech and even prose as a means for poetic expression. During the height of modernism, these two goals had never come to a synthesis. In this connection, I would like to point out that, in a significant way, the convergence of transparency and indeterminacy found in Chinese poetry has played an important role in promoting the use of montage and juxtaposition in modern film and poetry.

Now, turning to the Chinese scene, we find some strikingly similar activities with entirely different aesthetic and cultural causes and implications. The crisis of consciousness in modern China did not directly evolve from science, although, in an apocalyptic way, it was also related. The Chinese crisis can be briefly summarized as follows: the Western gun-boats (product of Western science), in an unprecedented move of material and ideological aggression, had driven China to the end of the rope, putting her intellectuals into a love-hate relationship with both traditional and Western structures of consciousness. This, we would like to argue, had created a uniquely local crisis of identity that had helped to forge what one may call a Chinese Hamletism apart from, and before the advent of Western modernism.

Under the crushing aggressions of the Western powers which brought about the fear of total destruction of China and unspeakable national disgrace, many writers came upon the historical arena with trepidation, diffidence and even shame, as if the once inviolable glory of China had been reduced to a midget to be laughed at, as if all the artistic and literary refinement she once possessed, became nothing but a source of barbaric expression. (Little did they know that, at this juncture of time, the Chinese language had been proclaimed as the most poetic language of all by Pound and others!)

If we should characterize Western modernism as an attempt to free man from being dominated by the reductive and distortive culture industry, the May 4th Movement which began with a radical rejection of the past and the almost undifferentiating adoption of Western alternatives, was meant as an attempt to free the Chinese from domination by the land-seizing and rights-taking Western powers and by native despotic institutions.

As we have already mentioned, intellects and artists in China and in the West at this time took opposite courses, and so in the beginning, we find almost no similarities in formalistic markers. Indeed, the Chinese counterparts initially adopted what the Western modernists had rejected just when the latter greatly prized the aesthetic strategies of classical Chinese poetry. There are many more examples of this intriguing interchange. Parallel to syntactical departures mentioned earlier, we find the West moving from perspective to diffusion of perspective when China took up the reverse course, abandoning traditional diffusion of perspective for the earlier Western counterpart. The impact of science upon consciousness was also quite different. The intellects in the West by this time were acutely aware of the traumatic consequences of science and were extremely critical of it while embracing it. The Chinese intellectuals during and after the May 4th movement avidly embraced science with practically no true understanding of what it had meant to the West. This, no doubt, was due to the fact that China had hardly any experience in industrialization, and therefore knew nothing about the threat of reification of the natural self.

The question of self in China had very different implications. In the May 4th Period, it was because of the reaction against the residual distortive and suppressive acts of the despotic imperial rule that the Western idea of self, under the rubric of democracy and liberalism, was first promoted. Hence, the popularity of self-analysis in the confessional novels of Yu Dafu and in the diaries of various poets. Hence, the ego–celebration of Guo Moruo. This ego trip was soon rejected in the 1930s through a rethinking of the Daoist concept of *chiwu*, or the equality of things, and the Confucian concept of *datong*, or great harmony. Meanwhile in the West, the self dominated, in spite of Eliot's claim of impersonality. Only a few later modernists (e.g., Williams, duBuffet and Snyder) were authentically interested in a Chinese type of selflessness.

In the midst of these differences and an intriguing interchange, we also see a significant convergence: the breaking of a unified world view leading to a distrust of the past and a search for new surrogates. In China, the breaking of the old order was not caused by an implosion of the hermeneutically fortified power structure that Copernicus and Galileo began in the West. China was initially incapacitated by Western gun boats before the intellectuals saw clearly both the implications of the native despotic domination and the liberating as well as dominating powers of science, the latter understood differently—the idea of ossification and reification not being part of the nuances for the Chinese intellectuals in this period. Like the West, even though the material causes were different, China was driven into a state of bewilderment equally traumatic. Indeed, as we will see later, the horizons of the new searches and the psychological conditions of the Chinese poets and intellectuals bore some rather striking resemblances.

Another similar activity must be mentioned here before we proceed further. Both the Western and the Chinese poets at this time advocated natural speech as a medium for expression, but for different ends. In the West, it was against the falsifying rhetoric of the nineteenth-century residual aristocracy. In China, partly influenced by the Imagists of the West, partly spurred by local necessity to change, the Chinese also talked about the falsifying rhetoric of the classical Chinese language which was still very much the property of the educated, and proposed *baihua* or plain speech as its substitute, but in China, it had an added need. In order to come to grips with the new external threat, the new medium was intended to disseminate democratic ideas to the populace. Hence, the tendency toward discursiveness in the beginning.

One central question remains to be answered: what is the *situatedness* in China that has made modernism possible in the midst of all these significant differences? The answers are two: (1) China was and still is facing what I have preferred to call a hermeneutical or interpretive crisis; (2) cross-cultural awareness of the paradoxes and ambiguities of the above issues has led poets of the 1940s and 1960s to revive classical Chinese strategies to supplement those of the West. The second answer must be reserved for another paper. Let us deal with the first.

Both the West and China had been driven into an exilic condition by different forms of domination: the West by increasingly instrumental, separatist, and divisive reasoning, and China by a combined native and foreign aggression. When I said earlier that the Chinese intellectuals had been driven into a love-hate complex, it means that they at once loved and hated Chinese and Western traditions. They were proud of the high culture of China but at the same time disdainful of China's corruptive, unself-reflexive institutions. They hated the hegemonic aggression of the Western powers which had brought China to the brink of extinction but could not help embracing Mr. Democracy and Mr. Science as if these two could indeed help resurrect China. But exactly where could they locate the truly cohesive form (hermeneutical and explanatory framework) for the beaten and beat China? What kind of cohesive form could they borrow from the West (if indeed there were such a thing!) to regenerate a vigorous China? These are still unanswered questions in the midst of a still uncured love-hate complex, in spite of many quests and questionings. (I need not point out here that "quests and questionings" form one of the most distinctive characteristics of modernism, i.e., an odyssey for knowledge).

In point of fact, ever since the May 4th movement as a reaction against domestic and foreign aggression and domination, Chinese intellectuals have been exiled into a cultural vacuum, each of them being left to embark on an odyssey for new knowledge, seeking, hesitating, expecting (for a new sign which never seems to come), questing, questioning, and getting lost in some abyss. As Lu Xun said in his "Shadow's Farewell," "But I don't want to hesitate between light and shade; I'd rather sink into darkness. And yet, I eventually have to hesitate between light and dark." He was the first poet to voice this desperate condition. He wanted to find a "sign" upon the tombstone, but instead, there were only broken fragments: "There is a soul which has been transformed into a snake full of poisonous teeth. Instead of biting others, it bites itself." Not only the poet, but also the people and the nation, had turned inward to a deep self-agony. "He takes out his heart to eat and tries to find out its taste. As he eats, it is too painful to know its true taste . . . but when the pain is gone and as he tries to eat it slowly, his heart is already spoiled, how can he know the true taste?" How can we know the true taste of Chinese culture? This represents indeed, the throes and pangs of Chinese culture after its Chineseness has been exiled into the wilderness.

For a similar reason, Wen Yiduo's poems are full of death-wish motifs: to die so as to be reborn! "Why not allow it to rot more / till the rotting cracks open my kernel, my prison / so that my shut-in soul / now wearing a bean–green vest, / can smilingly jump out."

The cultural vacuum has directly affected the vacuum of the self. Witness this poem by Mu Dan (1940):

> Cut off from the womb, all warmth lost,
> I am a torn part yearning for rescue,
> Always a single self locked in wilderness.
>
> From still dreams I left the group,
> And pained in time's flow, clutching at nothing.
> Continuous memories cannot bring back myself.
>
> The metamorphosed image is deeper desperation,
> Always a single self locked in wilderness,
> Hating mother for parcelling out a separate dream.

It was against this exilic condition resulting from a sudden interregnum of Chinese culture, against an equally oppressive threat of the disintegration of the natural self driven by a double violence, that the Chinese poets, willy-nilly, first embarked onto a self-agonizing quest for a cohesive center, which seems to be forever irredeemable. They hoped that if and when this center were resurrected, the scattered limbs could perhaps be pieced together again into which a new soul could be breathed. Such was and still is the prototypical *Angst* of Chinese modernism. Such is perhaps also that of other Oriental counterparts.

Notes

1. See my "The Use of 'Models' in East-West Comparative Literature," *Tamkang Review* 6.2 and 7.1 (October 1975–April 1976:109–126); "The Framing of Critical Theories; A Reconsideration," *Asian Culture Quarterly* 15.3 (1986): 29–39. See also my "Introduction" to *Comparative Literature Studies Series* (in Chinese), published by Tung-tai Press of Taipei (1983).
2. *Comparative Literature Studies* 11.1 (1974), or my *Bijiao Shixue* (Comparative Poetics) (Taipei: Tung-tai, 1983) 27–85.
3. See, for example, the sophisticated discussion in Althusser's "Contradiction and Overdetermination," in *For Marx*, trans. Ben Brewster. (New York: Vintage Books, 1970) 89–128.
4. See in particular the first two chapters in Voloshinov's *Marxism and the Philosophy of Language* (Reprint by Cambridge, MA: Harvard University Press, 1986).
5. "Transcoding Gadamer," a paper read in the Symposium on Culture, Literature and History held in Taipei, July 15–28,1987; hosted by National Tsing Hua University.
6. Jean-François Lyotard, *The Postmodern Condition* (1979), trans. Geoff Bennington and Brian Massumi (Minneapolis: University of Minnesota Press, 1984).

II. Language Strategies and Historical Relevance in the Poetry of 1930–1950

If literary and art works are responses to crises of consciousness, the poetry emerging from the modern period in China represents one of the most complex forms of antagonistic symbiosis brought about by the battles and negotiations between native sensibility and alien ideologies since the nineteenth century when the aggressive acts of Western gunboats attempted to colonize China.

Before we examine some of the Medusian ways in which this symbiosis has taken form, a word must be said first about the condition of colonization in China. While it is true that China has never been totally colonized by foreign powers, and although the four elements (as suggested by Albert Memmi)[1] that make up the stamp of an authentic cultural identity, namely, historical consciousness, sense of community, religious or cultural awareness, and language, have not been wiped out as they were in some of the African tribal societies, the colonizing activities of the Western and later the Japanese powers have clearly left indelible marks in modern Chinese culture. These include the centralization of alien cultures and the marginalization of indigenous traditions under the often divisive and subversive military and economic acts of aggression of the West, resulting in what Renato Constantino[2] called "cultural inauthenticity." The centralization comes in the form of unconscious assimilation or internalization of foreign structures of consciousness, including taste in music, film, art and literature, cultural theories and philosophies, clothing, as well as modes of production and distribution, class stratifications and socio-psychological ambiences. The result of this process is the desensitization of indigenous traditions: the relegation of things Chinese, the most obvious case being classical Chinese music, thus creating an invisible block to the intellectuals to rethink diacritically what exactly happens in a crosscultural confrontation. For example, few have been able to tell exactly what has been rejected in the iconoclastic movements, and exactly what has remained untouched, and how this untouched part of the Chinese tradition can help to mediate and negotiate with those non-dominating elements from the West to effect a synthesis that would consolidate and enrich, but *not overwhelmingly change*, the native intellectual horizon.

Many Western writers of modern Chinese history have diplomatically chosen the axes of "Western Impact and China's Responses," or "Tradition and Modernity" to frame their narratives. This is, of course, to downplay the derogatory implications of colonization, but it does not take long for any reader of modern Chinese history to find out that while full colonization has indeed not taken place, colonizing attempts have been active from the nineteenth century to at least as late as the 1940s, if not later.

Beginning with the notorious Opium War in 1839 which resulted in Hong Kong being ceded to Great Britain, China had been forced to open all the economically and strategically vital coastal ports to the West, signing off territorial and jurisdictional rights to Britain, France, Russia, Germany, Japan, Portugal and the United States, almost at the pace of a piece a year with special privileges extended. These Concessions remained in full force even as late as the 1940s, creating pockets of colonies all over China in key coastal metropolitan cities such as Shanghai where the Chinese suffered unprecedented humiliation. In the words of Hang Yuehe:

> This is Shanghai—sister of New York, London,
> Paris! Look! Overtaking us
> In striding fashion are those aliens,
> Brown hair, green eyes, once
> Masters here. We followed them and
> Turned with them on a gray sand road, and
> Learned to be "gentlemen" under their
> Conductor's rod, in a dark room,
> And thus: the following outrageous signboard must be taken down:
>
> CHINESE AND DOGS ARE NOT ALLOWED!
>
> Today, we want to come back as masters here. . . .

II. Language Strategies and Historical Relevance

Indeed, even after the Republic was established in 1911, taking advantage of a still feeble and untutored government, foreign powers continued territorial, jurisdictional, economical, and ideological aggressions. Take the May 4th Movement. One must be reminded that the massive, nationwide demonstrations and strikes on January 18, 1919, were provoked by the Versailles Peace Conference in which it was revealed that the Great Powers, for whom the Chinese intellectuals had placed high hopes for a just treatment, had secretly agreed earlier to Japan's claims. Japan had seized the German Concessions in Shandong in 1914 and had served China the notorious Twenty-one Demands in 1915 which included, among other things, Japanese control of Manchuria (which was later colonized), Inner Mongolia, Shandong, China's northeast coast, and the Yangtze Valley (= colonization of China!), employment of Japanese advisors in political, financial, and military affairs, Japanese ownership of land for hospitals, schools and churches, joint Sino-Japanese organizations (e.g., police), China to buy from Japan 50% or more of ammunitions, etc.! Take the May 30th Incident in 1925. Another series of massive, nationwide demonstrations and strikes were provoked , this time, by brutalities done to the Chinese citizens in the Concessions in Shanghai. The guards of a Japanese textile factory who killed a Chinese worker, instead of being brought to justice, were given protection by the British police who in turn killed more people, leading to over twenty foreign warships and marines of five nationalities landing on Chinese land, not unlike the aggressive acts of the Allied Forces occupying Peking in 1900! I need not mention here the well-known fact that in 1937 the Japanese invaded China and began eight years of brutality across half of China, including the notorious Nanking mass massacre.

But the alien powers were not the only adversary that the Chinese were faced with. The attraction to and the repulsion by the alien powers and ideologies were conditioned and complicated by the centuries-old oppressive and distortive hierarchical feudalistic system against which the Chinese intelletuals had to revolt, but which seemed to continue to have a lasting grip upon institutional and societal forms long after the May 4th advocacy of Mr. Democracy and Mr. Science.

One can now understand that the Chinese intellectuals' search for a new cultural rationale would necessarily take on a Medusian dimension, as Lu Xun's "Such a fighter" suggests. My scenario for this search (subsuming the above brief narratives) consists of at least the following: 1) highly emotional iconoclastic attacks on the Confucian autocratic monarchy, on the uncreative economy run by the gentry class which had totally alienated the poverty-stricken peasantry, on the feudal familial and societal customs and forms, as well as on classical language, literature and thoughts which had once brought the monolithic Middle Kingdom supreme glory; all this in the hopes of reestablishing China through institutional and social reforms and in the name of a "renovation of the Chinese people"; 2) the early attempts to provide surrogates for the deposed culture and simultaneous transplantation (often indiscriminately) of liberalism, utilitarianism, pragmatism, individualism, Darwinism, Ibsenism (emancipation of women, in particular), Socialism, Marxism, Neoclassicism, Romanticism, Symbolism, Aestheticism, Naturalism, Realism, Futurism, Expressionism, Dadaism, Revolutionary Literature, Proletarian Literature, etc., almost in one breath, sometimes with several trends converging upon one author; 3) the ensuing conflicts and debates over the question of "Chinese spirit" and "Western substance" which underline other debates: self/society, national form/regional form, realism/modernism, folk forms/modern metrical forms, etc.; 4) Running through these drastic changes were inbred violent events: the rapid destruction and unprecedented humiliation of the once inviolable China by the Western aggressors causing the Chinese to lose their national confidence which seemed (and still seems to many now) to be irrecoverable; the ineffectual national resistance to the alien powers resulting in blood-baths and national disgrace, pushing China to the brink of final demise; a series of self-awakening revolutions (political, cultural, literary) uniting the intelligentsia, the students and the workers in street demonstrations and strikes (May 4th, May 30th); 5) In the midst of all these interpenetrating historical events and changes in consciousness, the modern Chinese intellectuals are constantly caught in a love-hate complex with both traditional and Western cultural modes.

Against this fabric, a host of responses and dialogues arose, sometimes in diametrically opposed directions, very much the way the

II. Language Strategies and Historical Relevance

various isms emerged side-by-side in the 1920s as if on a slate with their various histories erased so that, like props on a new stage, they played out their roles to fit into a new history which is contemporary China. It is as if the Chinese intellectuals had felt, as never before, that China had reached the end of her rope. There was no time to think through both the Chinese and the Western systems to carefully work out a politico-socio-cultural framework best suited to the indigenous temperament. In the midst of their revolutionary zeal, what they saw was the potential of salvation which the various Western ideologies, collectively, seemed to promise, as if all of them, at root, were Promethean and Faustian. As we look back upon this period, in particular, the 1920s, the minds of almost all the intellectuals were colored by an explosive emotionalism. Thus, their works must not be read, as I have argued in the first essay, by putting them against the stylistic markers as we understand them in the West, but rather, we must see them in light of their *perception* and their *appropriation* of Western strategies as a function of their anxiety and of their attempt to come to grips with the crumbling chaos in their search for a *raison d'etre*. One thing is also clear from this fabric: the intensities—anxieties, solitudes, hesitations, doubts, nostalgia, expectancy, exile and dreams—of the Chinese writers rarely come from an insulated private space; they are at once intensely inward-personal and outward-historical, because they cannot help but be dialectical transfigurations from tensions and agonies of acculturation under the visible and invisible forces of colonizing activities. Like the works of most Third World writers, they cannot help but be explicitly or implicitly *critical*, as the examples at the end of my first essay of this introduction have amply illustrated.

* * *

Between consciousness and the world, there can be as many orientations towards natural phenomena, men and events as make up the fabric of reality. But, comparatively speaking, a great percentage of classical Chinese poetry tends to emphasize the relationships between man and nature whereas modern Chinese poetry, particularly in its inception, tends to focus upon those between the individual and society. Viewing natural phenomena as they are, as concrete particulars, as self-generating, self-transforming, self-regulating, self-conditioning, and self-sufficient forms of being, the classical Chinese poet often tries to avoid intellectual interference, to avoid projecting his subjectivity into them. Instead, he wants to return to a natural measure with things in their prepredicative condition, i.e., to allow them to disclose themselves relatively freely, believing as he does that man is only one among a million things that make up the total fabric of reality and, as such, he has no right to solely dominate and constitute them according to his subjective interests. The classical Chinese poets seldom put "I" in the primary position for aesthetic contemplation. This is not hard to understand: phenomena do not need "I" to have their own existences; they all have their own inner lives, activities and rhythms to affirm their authenticity as things. Subject and object, principal and subordinate, are categories of superficial demarcation. A thing can be both object and subject. Positions can be freely changed—subject and object, consciousness and phenomena inter-penetrate, inter-complement, inter-define, and inter-illuminate, appearing simultaneously, with men corresponding to things, things corresponding to things, extending throughout the million phenomena. To achieve this inter-disclosing relationship calls for a series of language strategies, such as those outlined in the first essay, including the flexibility of syntax that can leave the reader-viewer in an "engaging-disengaging" relationship with the world given to him, the diffusion of distances to make revolving perspectives possible as well as the use of negative space as a departure for the retrieval of the undifferentiated whole.

When the modern Chinese poet turns his attention toward the relationships between the individual and society, these cardinal questions arise: should he point toward an ideal society and relegate the individual? Should he privilege the unrestrained outpouring of his thoughts and feelings at the expense of society? What kind of society can be considered "ideal"? How to define an individual who is supposed to be free from the distortive fetters of social norms? There is little consensus on these questions. Conceptions of "ideal society" and "reasonable individual" constantly undergo changes with varying historical conditions. But almost all the writers wrestling with the question of the individual in society begin with some form of utopian vision, vague sometimes it may be, in order to criticize a society in question. But should this utopian vision behind the Chinese writers' consciousness arise from the Western brand of liberalism with roots reaching back to a post-Enlightenment hierarchical system solidified by instrumental reason and self-centeredness? Or should it work from a reconsideration of the relationship between man and nature, to see man as only a component in the cooperative design of the total composition of things?

In the inception of the modern period, however, many of these questions were hardly articulated, let alone expressed or answered. Listen to this poem by Guo Moruo,

> THE HEAVENLY HOUND
> I am the "Heavenly Hound."
> I ate up the Moon.
> I ate up the Sun.
> I ate up all the stars.
> I ate up the whole whole Universe.
> I am I.
> I am the light of the Moon.
> I am the light of the Sun.
> I am the light of all the stars.
> I am the light of X-ray.
> I am the total energy of the entire universe.
>
> I fly, I roar, I burn.
> I burn like fierce fire
> I roar like the sea.
> I run like electric power.
> I fly, I run, I fly.
> I skin myself.
> I eat my flesh.
> I drink my blood.
> I chew my heart.
> I run on my nerves.
> I run on my spines.
> I run on my brain-tissues.
> I am I.
> The I of I is going to explode.
>   –1920

The megalomania in this poem, with both the natural and the industrial worlds overwhelmed by the explosive language of an ego, contrasts sharply with the quiet correspondences of things or the withdrawal of the ego to allow the acting out in nature so characteristic of classical Chinese poetry (as in the examples of Wang Wei and other landscape poets). In this explosion of the ego, the consideration of language as an art is taken over by unrestrained passion. In the words of Wen Yiduo,

> Their (Guo and his group called Creationists) whole purpose is to expose their very *self*. All these self-pitying youths think the most beautiful object in the world is their self. When they have nakedly and unreservedly exposed their *self*, to them, this is a big success. Do you not see them singing every day the tune of "self-expression?" Indeed, they recognize only the raw materials of literature, but not the tool with which these materials are turned into art. It is almost accidental that they should use words as an expressive tool. The happiest thing for them is the so-called "self-exposure," to let the world know how "I", too, am a versatile youth, capable of elegant sickness and skilled at refined sadness. . . . with always a few drops of sentimental tears! Ho! Ho! Ho! How interesting! How romantic! Yes, romantic, their version of Romanticism! "Romantic," not to be confused with literary Romanticism!
> From "The Metrical Form of Poetry" (1926)

Now, in the words of Guo himself in two letters to his friend Zhong Baihua:

> Goethe once said, When the impulse of poetry came to him, he would run to his desk and, without taking time to straighten out the paper that was lying awry, he would scribble down everything from beginning to end. . . . I am most disgusted with forms and seldom spend time in forging them. What I write is from my sudden impulse, like going into a frenzied dance as it comes to me. (1920)

II. Language Strategies and Historical Relevance

Two observations must be made here. First, as I mentioned in passing in the first essay, Guo's ego-celebration, his friend Yu Dafu's confessional novels (modeled after the Japanese "I"-novels) and the popularity of the writers' diaries during the 1920s are part of the initial search for freedom from the residual distortive and suppressive acts of despotic imperial rule. In their eyes, the romantic emphasis on self is at root revolutionary, and as such, is most needed in this historical juncture as part of an overall iconoclastic movement. Second, this alliance with Romanticism must not be seen as their having any root understanding of Romanticism as it originally emerged in the West. They often highlighted only the emotional side of Romanticism (often in the extreme form of sentimentalism) and hardly understood the activities of imagination so central to the Romantics.

The initial responses to the political-cultural crises of China were mixed: excitement over a new China about to come, anger over the grip of power upon the masses and over the imperialistic colonizing activities, anguish and anxiety over the question of Chineseness, fervor for revolutionary action, desperation over the impasse Chinese culture had come to, etc. For the sake of convenience, let us examine three broad early configurations at the crossroads of the old and the new.

The first may be described as literature of premature optimism, or prospective literature in which the poet focuses his attention upon the future. Now that the old is considered dead, suddenly the poet finds himself standing in front of a vast new panorama, as if all the bright future is already *here* and *now*, viewing the surging clouds in the air, the rolling and pounding waves of the sea, the pulsation of the cosmopolitan (which has hardly arrived), indeed, all the activities in front of him, with a certain degree of positive affirmation, as if these new vistas were already in operation, dynamically, rhythmically, and ceaselessly forming one huge harmony, bright, unified, sublime, full of hope. The tone of the poet is ecstatic, passionate, celebrative with incantatory apostrophes and exclamations. But, in this way, the world is too much dominated and affected by the poet's overflowing subjectivity to be able to disclose itself objectively. The world that the poet celebrates is a potential world of the future projected onto the present and treated as if it were the immediate deliverance of experience. Guo Moruo, and many of the Creationist poets in the

1920s produced many poems of this kind. Take Guo's " Good Morning":

> Good morning! ceaselessly moving ocean!
> Good morning! lighted misty dawn!
> . . . .
> Morning winds! Please disseminate my voices to the four
>   corners of the world!
> Good morning! my young country!
> Good morning! my new-born brothers!

From here on, the poet salutes with similar apostrophes and format some twenty or so lands and peoples before concluding the poem with:

> Good morning! O Atlantic!. . . .
> O! O! Walt Whitman! Walt Whitman! Pacific-like Walt
>   Whitman!
> O! O! Pacific! . . .
> Quick! Come to enjoy this once-in-a-million-year dawn!

The almost sloganistic mode of expression infected many later action-oriented poets, in particular, poets that devoted themselves to revolutionary and proletariat causes. It was, in part, against the inundation of this sloganistic discursiveness that poets of the 1930s and 1940s made a special effort to rectify by rethinking the question of artistic language.

Interestingly, similar emotionalism and projections are reflected in the early work of a very different poet, Xu Zhimo of the Crescent Society, who, with Wen Yiduo, had, on various occasions, criticized the Creationists for their neglect of form and meter. Xu has a childlike naive faith in Love and in the power of Love which, he believes, can overcome all difficulties and reform the world. Like Guo, Xu has an unchecked overflow of emotion, an emotion also often carrying a positive tone—in his words, an "Everlasting Yea." Like Guo, his early poetry is full of off-the-ground ("carefree cloud-ride"), ethereal, intoxicating, dreamlike verbalizations of explosions of emotion. Apostrophes, repetitions, and exclamations abound. His, too, is a bright, misty, serene, boundless, distant world of the future projected onto the present. As such, it lacks a solid footing in the very complex reality of contemporary Chinese history, although a later Xu, with his emotion and his language in rein, has, together with Wen Yiduo, laid important grounds for some of the best poets of the 1930s and 1940s.

The second configuration emphasizes the present as it is. The works produced under this perceptual orientation have generally been considered as realistic. But in the case of the Chinese writers of the 1920s (and 1930s), almost all their works can be loosely called critical realism, because at heart, they aim at contesting the existing system in their praxis, and, representing the unfavored classes, they attempt to reorder the existing world by way of a call for its destruction. Thus, this literature can also be called protest literature. In modern China, although the form of government has already been changed from imperial rule to republican, the feudalistic repression in petrified forms of human relationships remains fully active. A writer in the present orientation would not simply accommodate himself to the system, but would necessarily raise a protest against the petrified relations under which he lives. Thus, we find that many writers, e.g., Lu Xun, Mao Dun, Lao Xie, Ba Jin etc., capitalize upon the distortion of the instinctive or natural self by these petrified relations and have produced significant representative novels delineating the complicating process of the making of the social self, including different levels of reification and fetishization.

When pitching the unfavored or oppressed classes against the favored or oppressing classes (including here the imperialist forces from outside, their native acccomplices, and native despotic institutions), a number of writers have unfortunately fallen into the pitfall of mechanical black-and-white typifications. Instead of pursuing the possibility of discovering the awakening of the natural self in an "oppressor," the latter is often too crudely characterized, and often with emotional brandishment, as wickedly aggressive. To be true to the actuality of the situation, one must understand that not all oppressors are born as aggressors; they are often led to behave so by a social system the hierarchical and territorizing activities of which have somehow veiled the very instinctive nature they might possess. The creation of middle characters to accommodate this variable is needed, but is often ignored. While their mechanical typifications of characters have led to inauthenticity, their emotional brandishment has precluded artistic consideration in the forefront of their writings. Both Lu Xun and Mao Dun have cause to remind their contemporary fellow-writers with these words: "All literature is propaganda, but not all propaganda is literature." (Lu Xun) "Only revolutionary passion cannot become literature." (Mao Dun)

The poetry that assumes this perceptual orientation often privileges the narrative form—story poems or lyrics with a strong storyline. As can be expected, a huge percentage of these poems, propelled by their impulse to call for action and reform, with the exception of those by Ai Qing and a few others, often fall flat for being overly prosaic and didactic. Like the formulaic novelists, too, they tend to idealize the unfavored classes at the expense of authenticity. Prosaism and inauthenticity are two of the evils the poets of the 1930s and 1940s have had to wrestle with. Witness these critiques by two poets of the 1940s:

> Although new Chinese poetry has only a short history of twenty years, it has already formed two traditions, i.e., two extremes! All that is done in one is : "O Dreams! O Roses! O Tears!"; all that is done in the other is: "O Rage! O Blood! O Bright Future!" The result is that the former takes leave of life, while the latter takes leave of art, thus, putting aside the sacred mission of combining life and art into a meaningful whole.
>
> Mo Gong (Chen Jingrong): "Sincere Voices,"
> *Shi Chuangzhao (Poetry Creation)* No.12. 1948.p.6.

Two prominent types of poetry emerge from recent works: one type aims at stating one's intentions or beliefs, hoping to effectively influence others' intentions or beliefs through poetry. Another aims to express a certain passion, hoping to affect others through poetry. The first type, with rather firm beliefs, often uses straightforward, strong language and fierce tones: "I want...," "We don't want ... ," " We advocate ... , " or "We oppose ...." The second, with clearly identified objects of love or hate, often begins with naked statements or protests. There is nothing wrong with stating intentions or expressing emotions which are major parts of life, and no doubt, major parts of poetry also, necessary and praiseworthy. But what is wrong with these

II. Language Strategies and Historical Relevance

two types of poetry, or rather their failure, lies not in their beginning intention nor in their end result . . . but in the process of turning intentions or feelings into poetic experience.
Yuan Kejia, "Dramatization in New Poetry,"
Shi Chuangzhao, No.12. 1948. p.3.

The third configuration is what can be called the poetry of identity crisis. Identity crisis arises when man is driven into some form of existential extremity or crisis, such as when he is in exile, finding himself cut off from a center of coherence, lost among shattered pieces, hesitating between the disintegrated past and the uncertain future. Solitary, anxious, nostalgic, and overwhelmed by a sense of futility and desperation, he turns inward to seek for a new *raison d'etre* by attempting, through creativity, to come up with a world (even if it be only aesthetic!) of new coherence for himself, and, in the case of modern China, also for Chinese culture. As we can now see, the prose poems of Lu Xun, the works of Wen Yiduo, and many works emerging from the 1930s and 1940s, examples of which I briefly mentioned at the end of the first essay of this volume, fall into this broad configuration. As I have said, "Ever since the May 4th Movement, as a reaction against domestic and foreign aggression and domination, Chinese intellectuals have been exiled into a cultural vacuum, each of them being left to embark on an odyssey for new knowledge, seeking, hesitating, expecting (for a new sign which never seems to come), questing, questioning,and getting lost in some abyss." The old culture and society is now denounced, discarded, and together with it the aesthetic dimension in the perception of reality. But is it that easy to swing a wisdom-sword to cut off the linking nets of affection for two thousand years of brilliant, and, as it has been *labeled* "exquisite" culture? And yet, modern Chinese historical developments are constantly urging poets to identify with the new culture. But where is the new center of cultural coherence? This yet-to-be-born new culture seems to be a mass of uncertainty. *To be or not to be*, that is the question.

Since the crisis of identity is both personal and cultural, bodily-existential and spiritually-aesthetical, the battles and negotiations address at once several fronts of contemporary Chinese metamorphosis. Hence, the attempts in many modern Chinese studies to privilege one direction, such as critical realism or revolutionary literature or socialist realism, at the expense of another, such as the socalled "aesthetic" school, or vice versa, have bypassed the uniqueness of the cultural metamorphosis in modern China. Strictly speaking, there is no aesthetic school in modern China, because the aesthetic strategies employed in the poems, and, for that matter, the choice of the aesthetic stance itself, already entail a battle between two modes of cultural consciousness, and are, therefore, always political. Indeed, without going through the complex process of confrontation, resistance, negotiation, modification, and /or fusion (in Fredric Jameson's sense, namely, maintaining a form of "tension, a coexistence within radical difference") between aesthetic and cultural forms, the new culture would emerge as merely an appendix to an ideology with a different center. What the poets of the 1930s and 1940s have offered represents precisely a period of reflection on a broad spectrum of clashes and tensions, including the appropriation of Western strategies and techniques through the confrontation, dialogue and interplay with those of classical China and an attempt to refine and energize the *baihua* or plain speech so that it can become as richly expressive as the *wenyan*, or classical Chinese language.

* * *

Due to the magnitude of the colonizing activities of foreign forces leading to the imminence of China's possible demise and the widespread poverty that plagued China from the very beginning, the Chinese poets found themselves hesitating between action and art.

> Let us break out from this suffocating,
> Nightmare-filled
>   illusive house,
> Leaving the trickery of words
> Behind doors. We go
> Onto the streets, onto the streets . . .
>   Hang Yuehe, "Resurrected Earth" (1948)

II. Language Strategies and Historical Relevance

It was wrestling with the dilemma between the need for action and the need for artistic creation that made several important poets decide to swing more toward action, or action-inspiring writings. In the late 1920s, advocates of revolutionary literature, people like Guo Moruo and Cheng Fangwu, outrightly proclaimed : "Action first, Art second," thus encouraging an inundation of sloganistic poetry. In the 1930s, with the acceleration of Japanese aggression and worsening living conditions in Northern China, poets who began as modernists like Ai Qing (who once indulged in Baudelaire, Rimbaud and Apollinaire) or as obsessive aesthetes like He Qifang, later modified and even abandoned the world of words to write exclusively for the proletariat. The manifesto poem of He Qifang is a case in point:

CLOUDS
"I love clouds . . . the clouds which pass by. . . . "
I thought of myself as that man in Baudelaire's prose poem
Who raised his neck melancholily
Looking into the distant sky.

I walked into the rural area.
Peasants lost their land because they were honest,
Their home reduced to a bundle of farming tools.
In the daytime, they went to the fields to find odd jobs.
At night, they slept on dry hard stone bridges.

I walked into the city by the sea.
Upon the tar streets of winter,
Rows and rows of apartments stand,
Like modern prostitutes upon sidewalks,
Waiting for pleasures of summer,
And pot-bellied lust and shamelessness.

From now on, I will make loud comments:

I'd rather have a thatched roof;
I don't love clouds, nor moon,
Nor stars.
    —1937

Indeed, leafing through the entire corpus of poetry of this period, similar statements abound. It has become a constant reminder to almost all the makers of beauty, prompting them from behind an arras. Thus, one of the aims of many of these poets is to strike a balance between the two. In the words of the poets who edited the *Zhongguo Xinshi (New Chinese Poetry)* (Fang Jing, Xin Di, Hang Yuehe, Chen Jingrong, Tang Qi and Tang Shi, most of whom are represented in this anthology):

> Everywhere is the thunderous call of history: Go to the wilderness, go to people's struggles . . . We are now standing in the wilderness, feeling the fast changes of winds and clouds. We must unfold the exploration of our thoughts with blooded and fleshed feelings. We must have full command of the voice of the age, and with dedicated seriousness execute our thoughts, first about ourselves, and then our solemn connectedness to all historical life . . . We must battle continuously not only with life, but also with art . . . We must possess an integrated style representative of the people and the times as well as a transcending perspective of history. We must allow unique and deepened individual styles that fit each differing personality. We must first form our own position as man in the river of history, i.e., to form one's poetic style in the creation of art. We must further demand of ourselves not to create a splendor of any self above and beyond that of an individual.
>
> Issue No. 1, June, 1948, pp.2–3.

There are three levels of dialectical relationship between life and art represented by poets that are of particular significance in this juncture of history.

1) These poets affirm that since man is rooted in history, he must respond to the call of history. Hence, almost all the poets of this period have written about wartime China. In fact, two outstanding poets of the 1940s, Mu Dan and Du Yunxie, had literally been embroiled in the painful experiences of war. Aside from war experiences, they have also written on the hardships of the Chinese people and the wretched state of the Chinese society.

2) They affirm the mutual dependence between an individual and history. A product of history, an individual should also be a maker.

3) They point out that the transition from the splendor of an individual to that of no self requires deep artistic consideration. To think, for a poet, is not an abstract, conceptual activity, but a process with "blooded and fleshed feelings", or, in Tang Shi's words, it is " to think with the sensory organ of one's body", as he paraphrases Bian Zhilin's "sensuality" and Eliot's "objective correlative" or "emotional equivalent".

One central issue that keeps recurring from the critiques by Lu Xun, Wen Yiduo and Mao Dun of the 1920s to the poetic statements of the 1940s is the question of the making of artistic language. All the critics agree that there is no spontaneous nightingale in the writing of poetry. The classic story about the poets of the Tang Dynasty who spent days and days trying to come up with a word to energize a line of poetry the way the dotting of the eyes of a painted dragon on the wall would make it fly away is still the lesson to be learned for any one who takes the writing of poetry seriously. The making of "the eye of the line," as it is called in classical Chinese poetics, has been actively pursued by both action-oriented and art-oriented poets. Take the example of Zhang Kejia, a self-declared action-oriented peasant poet. This is the way in which he explains the making of the first two lines of his "Refugees":

> I have never allowed myself to relax in the Hammering and forging of words and verses . . . . Take the first two lines of my "Refugees":
>
> The sun has fallen into the birds' nests.
> The afterglow has not yet dissolved the wings of returning
>   crows.
>
> At first, I wanted to write: "In the afterglow are flapping wings of returning crows"; later I changed it to "In the afterglow, one can still tell the returning crows' wings." Finally, I decided on the present form. I think the last version is better. Just close your eyes and visualize. The afterglow in the dusk is blurred. A skyful of colors of the afterglow deepen minute by minute and the wings

of the crows thin out minute by minute. Finally, both become indistinguishable as if the wings of the crows were dissolved by the afterglow . . .

    Zhang: "Tidbits from my experience as a poet" 1955.

The making of the "eye," the line, and finally the poem required the poets of this period to refine the *baihua* as a medium for expression. As we have already observed, when the *baihua*, or plain speech, was promoted during the May 4th Movement to replace the literary or classical Chinese, the need to disseminate democratic ideas to the populace precluded other artistic considerations. As such, it departed significantly from the classical Chinese poem's dominantly dramatic and cinematically visual presentation of things relatively free from the domination of the garrulous ego. (See the list of stylistic features of the classical Chinese poem discussed on pages 3–4.) The didactic impulse takes over with constant intrusion of the personal pronoun.

 The analytical tendency of the *baihua* was perhaps the result of several factors. First, inherent discursiveness. Before the poets adopted the *baihua* as a medium, it had been exploited largely by the novelists; all the poems found in the novels were written in classical Chinese, and when a moment of poetic intensity arose, the novelists turned to classical Chinese lines of poetry for assistance rather than trying to make the *baihua* poetic. And the novel, as a linear structure, emphasized logical developments and causal relations and operated with many analytical elements. When the poets adopted the medium, all the discursiveness came with it. The situation was worsened by the intrusion of Western sciences, systems of logic and forms of poetry. The *baihua* is being Europeanized (as the Chinese called it) in the process of translation (both journalistic and literary.) Efforts were made to fit the Procrustan bed by the introduction of Occidental syntax and the adoption of foreign grammatical frameworks as bases to explain, if not form, the Chinese sentence and the application of punctuation to regulate and clarify linguistic structures. All these were intended, no doubt, to show the hegemonic West that we have just as much logic and are just as scientific as the West, as if poetic ambiguity and richness were a shame!

 The steps taken to refine the *baihua*, however, should not begin by reverting to the classical Chinese language, for to do so would

II. Language Strategies and Historical Relevance

defeat the new culture, by reappropriating it through a process of tensional modifications.

One such modification is to combine classical Chinese phraseology with the *baihua*. Some early attempts have been quite awkward, such as that found in the poetry of Li Jinfa which comes to us with the feeling of a language undigested in spite of some startlingly bold and original images. But beginning with poets like Bian Zhilin and Xin Di, more successful syntheses emerge, a preparation for later poets to construct a more pregnant poetic medium.

A second step in the refinement process is to decrease the intrusion of the didactic impulse so as to allow more events, in dramatic and visual presentation, to play out their fates before the reader. Indeed, the dramatic and the cinematically visual presentation becomes the best strategy to offset the often dry and domineering didactic. A good example is Ai Qing's "Snow Falls on the Land of China", in which the commentary on the brutal events of war upon the poverty-stricken northern Chinese is transformed into a voice which is spoken as a role upon a stage prepared by a series of highly suggestive and symbolic cinematic shots (first by panning and then by zooming in):

> Snow falls on the land of China
> Cold locks the entire nation . . .
>
> Wind,
> Like an old woman too sorrowful
> Following closely at our heels
> Stretches her cold claws
> Pulling at the clothes of passers-by
> And with words ancient as earth
> Ceaselessly mumbles
>
> Emerging from the woods
> Hurrying horse-carts along
> You, peasants of China
> Wearing a leather hat
> Bracing the heavy snow
> Where are you going?

Let me tell you. . . . . . .

The tensional modifications in the process of language refinement have taken several directions: rhythmic interplay, the making of atmosphere, meditative deployment of events, the art of attention, and structural dialogue.

Dai Wangshu is one of the first poets to attempt a synthesis of rhythmic and motif interplay between the Chinese *ci* (poems of long and short lines written according to tone-patterns of musical tunes in the Song Dynasty) and the poetry of Verlaine. Indeed, Dai's "The Alley in the Rain", which describes a dreamy, momentary encounter of a lilac-like girl in the alley in the rain, fulfills almost everything Verlaine's "Art Poetique" proposes: "Music before everything . . . the Uneven, more vague and soluble in the air with nothing weighty or stable . . . Nuance, the play of light and shade." Musically, the repetitions and refrains closely echo Verlaine's "Chanson d'Autumne." A Chinese reader would also immediately hear echoes from the Chinese *ci*, not only the motif resemblance to the Chinese line, "The lilac knots in vain the ennui in the rain", but also the perfumed shadows and hushed melodies so typical of the *ci* poems. The invocation of the *ci* form (long and short lines) is also meant to find a middle ground between rigid metrical forms (classical Chinese poetry; the Crescent poets of the 1920s) and the unrestrained *vers libre* of Guo Moruo's variety, to bring to it a flow, easy-going but musically controlled. This flow Dai calls "the music of moods."

Like Dai, Xin Di and He Qifang also modify their verse with the rhythm and sensibility of *ci*, but Xin Di and He Qifang appeal also to the making of atmosphere in distinctive images. Here is Xin Di's "Afternoon in Autumn":

> Sunlight is like rolls & rolls of torn silk.
> Upon the pane is reflected the cold, white distant river.
> Those slender slender
> Hands of insects feet of insects
> How much coldness do they pick up?
> The light of year gradually goes.
> 1936

II. Language Strategies and Historical Relevance

The visual transparency achieved here is not unlike that of classical Chinese landscape poets, e.g., Xie Lingyun (385–433) and Xie Tiao (464–499). Compare it with Xie Tiao's "Transparent river is quiet like silk", or Xie Lingyun's "Sky-water both clear and fresh." With the exception of the last line, which is an afterthought, the poem also works typically like a classical Chinese poem. Against a wide expanse of natural scenery is juxtaposed the activity of some small forms of life in a co-extensive and inter-disclosing manner. The synaesthetic image of torn silk, the cold, white distant river, and the slender hands and feet of insects upon the pane are images that suggest a series of possible significations above and beyond their visual, physical appearance as such.

We must note here that the images that retain their openness to interpretive entrances can only be captured in a mode of consciousness in which there is no hurry-scurry to establish causal relations so as to let each moment emerge in its full distinctiveness before commentary intrudes. In this mode of consciousness, the poet is either absorbed in a trancelike contact with objects, in which the poet seems to be able to see or hear activities one is not normally aware of, or in a meditative attentiveness upon the objects, following their cuts and turns as they unfold themselves in their natural measure, including their position, distance, tone, thickness of color and light, direction and tempo of their movement, elements any successful camera shot must attend to.

Feng Zhi, Bian Zhilin, Xin Di, Zheng Min and Du Yunxie all capitalize upon this trancelike or meditative attention on objects as their main threshold to disclose the natural measure of things as they emerge before us.

Feng Zhi is a master of the art of attention to detail. Unlike some of his predecessors who cry over fire, blood, wars, brimming with anger and tears, Feng Zhi, like the earlier Rilke whom he once studied, aims at presenting ordinary things as significant existences, "things . . . around us / That demand our re-discovery" (Sonnet 26). He observes ordinary people, things, and events with pure love patiently, humbly, listening to their voices and silences and slowly discloses their destinies usually ignored by the larger world. Like the Daoist who puts all forms of beings on an equal footing and affirms each of the myriad things as solemn, beautiful, inter-dependent and inter-defining, Feng Zhi seeks to disclose them in moments of their epiphany, not by the tour-de-force of imagination, but by dedicated, patient attention to their emergence and their activities, to release them from their seeming irrelevance to become relevant within an aura of intimacy. Take his Sonnet 23, which delineates the simple act of a mother dog mouthing her newborns to receive sunshine after half a month of ceaseless rain and mouthing them back after sundown. The way in which Feng captures this simple event patiently, attentively, and ritualistically allows us to cross over from the practical to the domain of the sacred, into the whatness of the moment's interior, thus feeling a sense of infinity from finite objects. What is particularly important here is that, from beginning to end, we are not asked to go beyond the *here*, the *now* and the *real* into an artificial, abstract realm so much prized by Western metaphysics.

An extension of this mode of attention can be found in a kind of interior dialogue Zheng Min has with the objects disclosing themselves to a meditative and mediating consciousness:

> In the green sheen of earth and moss,
> I suddenly fall back into the world,
> Into a sinking mud pond.
> My eyes open, as it were,
> In the deep, dark night,
> And see clearly all things
> In their most secret moments.
> My ears
> Wake up suddenly
> And hear all things
> Speaking in the evening . . .
> . . . .
> But because people live their lives—
> Each to himself,
> I am reminded of
> One rock, another rock,
> One tree, another tree,
> A dream unparticipatible. . . .
>   "Loneliness"

II. Language Strategies and Historical Relevance

A very different kind of attention and attentiveness, keen, sharp, and arresting can be found in Du Yunxie's "Encampment":

> Tonight I suddenly discover
> In a tree a different beauty:
> It opens up for me
> A sky of pure, blue silk.
> . . . .
> . . . .
> A leaf wafts and falls down
> Like a face from afar.
> It hits the ground with a "zap."
> I hear then whispers of the wind.
> . . . . .

The images, with a leap of imagination, reflect the specificity of the conditions in which the poet's observations are made. The poet, stationed in a wartime outpost during the war resisting the Japanese invasion, begins the poem with a controlled, quiet, and slow description of the activities around him. He has to retain a special vigilance throughout the night. Any small movement will catch his unusual attention, hence, the falling leaf can be "a face from afar" as it hits the ground with a "zap" (Chinese *sha*, kill).

Contrary to the unchecked overflow or explosion of emotion of the poets of the 1920s, poets in the 1930s and 1940s offer a poetry of unhurried, controlled revelation of things and events, taking great care to allow them to complete their activities in accordance with the pregnancy, the measure and the curves of their orbit.

Of all the tensional modifications, the most sophisticated and most revealing in the way of inter-reflection and/ or cross-fertilization is the poetry of Bian Zhilin, whose theory, translations and practice have exerted great influence on the poets of 1940s, in particular, on the Nine Leaves poets (Xin Di, Chen Jingrong, Du Yunxie, Hang Yuehe, Zheng Min, Tang Qi, Tang Shi, Mu Dan and Yuan Kejia). We will not be able to retrace all the aspects of Bian's work here. Instead, we will examine only a short poem to show some aspects of the tensional interplay possible, and perhaps inevitable, explicitly or implicitly, in the symbiosis brought about by the confrontation of two modes of consciousness.

"FRAGMENT"
You stand upon the bridge to look at the landscape.
A landscape viewer upon the tower looks at you.

The moon decorates your window.
You decorate other people's dreams.

We know from his own translations of European works that he is very conversant with most of the symbolist and post-symbolist writings. He himself has once listed the poets that have influenced him: Baudelaire, Verlaine, Eliot, Yeats, Rilke, Valery, Auden, Aragon and Brecht.[3] His indebtedness to classical Chinese poetry and philosophy can easily be detected from the wording of his lines, which include, among other things, complete lines in classical Chinese neatly fitted into the *baihua*. It is not difficult to locate traces of influence here and there, but to do so would not help to reveal the uniqueness of his particular frame of mind.

"Fragment" looks, on the surface, very much like a Poundian poem of super-position, " one idea set on top of another." In some way, it even bears some resemblance to Pound's "Metro" poem, in which an image from the human world, " The apparition of these faces in the crowd," and an image from the natural world, "Petals on a wet, black bough" overlie and inter-define each other, a technique which has also been described as the montage Pound and others indirectly learned from China .[4] But the structural play is much more intriguing here. Bian is juxtaposing a Daoist perceptual horizon over a dubious counterpart. In my "Daoist Theory of Knowledge", I illustrate Zhuang Zi's idea of "Heaven and earth have their great beauties but do not speak of them" with Bian's first two lines which, I believe, embody the gist of Daoist thinking. To facilitate my discussion there, I added a third line, "Landscapes from all around look at you [them] both," following the suggestion of the first two lines. Let me quote this part in its entirety:

> *You* (perceiver) *stand upon the bridge* (definite position, using the so-called independent, self-sufficient subjective consciousness) *to look at* (to look at requires the setting up of distance; distance is a kind of depth, a precondition of looking in order to reveal the

II. Language Strategies and Historical Relevance

objects in question clearly) *the landscape* (the object being looked at.)

First, we must point out the precondition of perception and experience. To look at something requires distance, i.e., between subject (consciousness) and object (world); no perception is possible if there is no distance. In a real sense, when subject and object merge together, thought is no longer possible; when merged together, subject cannot look at object. On the other hand, distance will set up "definite position" and "definite direction", and will thus create biased and restrictive perception.

A *landscape viewer upon the tower* (another perceiver, another positioning, another subjective consciousness) *looks at* (another distance, another depth, another degree of clarity for objects to reveal themselves) *you* (perceiver becomes the perceived, and thus, the so-called independent, self-sufficient subjective consciousness is now broken.)

Landscapes from all around look at you both. (Different perceivers, different positionings, different distances with depths constantly undergoing changes and adjustments, and thus, breaking all definite, determinate positionings.)

Some observations are now in order:
a) To see or look already suggests that there is an object on the other end, even if the object is emptiness or void.
b) The Chinese character *jian* (見) captures better the true relationship between the subject and the object.
Jian (見) means to see or look at from here to there, from this to that, but also means to appear, to emerge, *xian* (現), i.e., the object discloses itself to us. We not only look at the scenery; the scenery also discloses itself to us, a "see—appear" simultaneity.
c) We are outside scenery (so that we can look at it), but we are also inside it (in which we are a part.)
d) Outside scenery, also inside it, scenery outside scenery, scenery within scenery—there is an inmeasurable silence among them with countless different distances and depths, a silence which is also a contract, a bond recognizable among themselves

that does not require our speaking about them. There is a condition of knowing, a kind of prepredicative, precoding, prelinguistic "needlessness to know".

e) Thus, when a scene enters our visual consciousness, it already brings with it the structure and history of this bond. This is the acting-out and weaving of Zhuang Zi's "Great beauties do not speak," and an innate knowledge before being dominated by subjective interests. There is a correspondence between objects and objects, a togetherness, a language before voice, a primitive and primary conversation waiting for us to learn, a music from Nature that blows upon the myriad things.

f) And this rich possibility of interdependent, inter-disclosing of objects depends upon the perceiver emptying out a free space, a void so as to co-exist with, rather than resist against, the perceived, forming a uniquely intimate community.[5]

As we can see, everything that is implicit in Bian's first two lines becomes a critique against the intruding ideology, the ego-domineering, goal-directed, one-dimensional, instrumental scientific thinking of the West. No chosen position or perceptual orientation should be privileged, because each position and perceptual orientation is territorialized by certain subjective interests and is hence restrictive and distortive. Each perceiving act must, therefore, be considered provisional. Now when we turn to the next two lines of Bian's poem,

> The moon decorates your window.
> You decorate other people's dreams.

we will find that beyond the rhetorical echoes and interplay, there is this added implicit commentary. Like the provisionality of each perceiving act, human activities are or should be seen as provisional and should not be seen as the final statement of some hegemonic value system.

As we can also see now, everything we have received from the West should go through a dialogue of this kind, "a preservation of tension, a co-existence within radical difference" and one should not be overwhelmed by the other. The native sensibility should not be allowed to be desensitized in the process of internalization of alien ideology. It is no accident that Bian, totally well-versed in Western literature, should quote the Daoist-derived Chan Buddhist lines "Green mountains, green. White clouds, white," i.e., each form of being should be left uninterfered with in its natural endowment, in his "Untitled II"; that he should rewrite Chapter 11 of *Dao-de-jing* ("Thirty spokes toward one hub;/ Empty center/ is wheel's use . . . etc.), the source of the Chinese aesthetics of Emptiness, into his own version of the same in his "Untitled V" ("Because it is empty. . . . Because it allows for your promenade.") It is equally no accident that he should have written such poems as "Composition of Distances," "Round Jewel-Box," and "White Shell," all involving changing perspectives, changing distances or reversing roles, all of a transformed Daoist horizon, as counter-discourses to other subject-dominated discourses, which he himself also practices, as a product of the new Chinese culture. It is this tensional dialogue between structures and horizons, more explicitly in Bian, and more hidden in others perhaps, that we must discover from the poetry of modern China—a new legacy for the world to meditate upon.

Del Mar, Ca.
1990.

Notes

1. Albert Memmi, *The Colonizer and the Colonized*, trans. Howard Greenfeld. (Boston: Beacon Press, 1967.)
2. *Neocolonial Identity and Counter-consciousness* (London: Merlin Press, 1978), p.165.
3. *Diaochong Jili*, expanded edition (Hong Kong: Joint Publications,1982), p.20.
4. See my article "Classical Chinese and Modern Anglo-American Poetry: Convergence of Languages and Poetics" in *Comparative Literature Studies* 11.1 (1974).
5. "The Daoist Theory of Knowledge" in *Poetics East and West*, ed. Milena Dolezelova-Velingerova, The Toronto Semiotic Monograph Series. No.4, 1988–89, pp. 62–3.

III. Literary Modernity in Chinese Poetry
by Leung Ping-Kwan

In the 1930s and 1940s in China, there emerged a generation of poets with a distinct modernist outlook. This generation followed the innovations of the first generation of Chinese New Poets in the foregrounding of the vernacular language and stylistic multiplicity and backgrounding of classical language and regulated form. The modernity of their work is shown by their breaking with traditional value judgments and representational emphases, their adversary stance to bourgeois and commercial culture, and their deviation from familiar codes of communication. This generation includes the poets who first appeared in poetry journals in the thirties, the central and representative one being *Xinshi* [New Poetry], published in Shanghai from 1935 to 1936. Their efforts were put to an abrupt end by the outbreak of war, but the poets continued to work in other interior areas not directly affected by war. One important center was Kunming, at *Xinan Lianda* [Southwest Associated University], where the teachers of literature were some of the best poets of the time and a group of students appeared who produced some memorable works during the time of the war. After the war, they and some others contributed to poetry journals and literary supplements of newspapers in Beijing and Shanghai in the late forties and introduced and translated Western modernist poetry. Although the Chinese poets shared many similar concerns with their Western counterparts, unique social and historical contexts, such as the Sino-Japanese War (1937–1945) and the post-war period of social and economic instability (1945–1949), shaped the particular morphology of the Chinese modernist poetry. However, because of their opposition to the dominant social and cultural trends of their time, this generation of poets was ignored by left and right political groups, and their works have not been anthologized or studied since the change of political atmosphere in

1949. It was only in the early eighties that their work began to be reprinted and some of them started to publish their poems again.¹

1. *Les Contemporains* and Its Claim for Modernity.

There had been early tentative attempts at literary modernity by the symbolist Li Jinfa and young poets from the late Crescent School like Bian Zhilin. But one group of writers who had consciously striven for literary modernity was centered around *Xiandai* [*Les Contemporains*] (1932–1935), a magazine published by Xiandai Shudian [Contemporary Bookstore] in Shanghai. Novelist and poet Shi Zhecun worked as editor for the first two volumes and co-edited with Du Heng beginning with the third volume.² Poets who had their works published in the magazine ranged from the symbolist Li Jinfa to the more politically oriented Guo Moruo, Zhang Kejia and Ai Qing. These poets did not actually form a school with definite literary policy. The name of the magazine in Chinese, *Xiandai*, can be translated as "modern" and keen efforts had been made to bring in modern Western literature with special emphasis on American poetry. Besides individual articles on and translations of Carl Sandburg, American woman poets, and the Imagists, there was a special issue on modern American literature. The poetry section in that issue included a general survey of modern American poetry, a sketch of Pound and his Imagist group, and translations of a group of poems by Robert Frost, E.A. Robinson, Amy Lowell, Conrad Aiken, Sara Teasdale, Carl Sandburg, Ezra Pound, H.D., John Gould Fletcher, Max Weber, Alfred Kreymborg, and Joyce Kilmer.³ This selection seems to have been indiscriminative in regard to quality and the discussion on these American poets is neither extensive nor theoretical. They were acclaimed as the creators of a new kind of poetry that portrays modern life in an unconventional poetic language. Thus poet and editor Shi Zhecun gives this picture of Sandburg:

> He sings of Chicago's skyscrapers, the fog, the canoe for outings, the sunset outside hotel windows, hoodlums, steelworkers, potato-diggers, men who husk maize. He sings of moors, jungles, railways, and roads. Like the American poet Walt Whitman before him, he breaks the traditional boundary in his choice of

poetic themes, utilizing all he sees and hears in daily contacts. His tones, like his themes, are also untraditional.[4]

The poet Shao Xunmei, in his introduction to American poetry, also emphasizes urban themes.[5] These themes and his selection of foreign poetry revealed his ideal type of poetry. In response to a reader's accusation that the poems in *Les Contemporains* were difficult to understand, Shi Zhecun said:

> The poetry in *Les Contemporains* is truly poetry; moreover it is purely modern poetry. It is the expression of modern sentiments that modern man experiences in contemporary life, written in modern language and framed in modern poetic form.
> What we call modern life consists of a variety of different aspects. The harbors crowded with steamers, the noisy factories, the subterranean mines, the squares ringing with jazz, the department stores in the skyscrapers, the battles of planes in the air, the spacious race courses . . . even Nature has changed considerably and is no longer what it used to be. In the midst of all these, can our poets still feel the same emotions as the previous generation?[6]

As for the issue of poetic technique, the editor, while defending the use of archaic diction by some of the poets, rejected attempts by poets from other groups such as *Xinyue* [Crescent poets], that followed the metrical form of Western poetry and dismissed its formulated rhyming schemes and stanzaic symmetry. Shi says:

> The poems in *Les Contemporains* frequently do not make use of rhymes. The lines are not even in measured lengths, but they all have rather fine texture; they are written in a modern form; they are true poetry![7]

Because of the polemic statements in this editorial, the poets from *Les Contemporains* have been since regarded as "Xiandai pai," [the Modernists School] in Chinese New Poetry.[8] This group provided a telling contrast to the modernists that came later. Although modern Chinese poetry of the early thirties as represented by *Les Contemporains* was interested in a kind of modernism that aimed at portraying modern urban life, the generation from the late thirties to the early forties was entirely different and more complicated in establishing itself as modernistic.

That the description of modern life does not guarantee a true spirit of modernity has been made clear by critics. Renato Poggioli, for example, warns us against a kind of superficial modernism that is a degeneration of modernity:

> Modernism leads up to, and beyond the extreme limits, everything in the modern spirit which is most vain, frivolous, fleeting and ephemeral. The honest-to-goodness nemesis of modernity, it cheapens and vulgarizes modernity into what Marinetti called encomiastically, *modernolatry*: nothing but a blind adoration of the idols and fetishes of our time.[9]

Such a wretched modernolatry, as seen by Poggioli, is a form of regression, a sort of provincialism:

> Provincial too appears to be the contemporary passion for urbanism and the urbanistic, the exaltation of the tentacular city, and the great capitals and industrial metropoles, where the crowd deludes itself into believing it lives a richer and more real life.[10]

In fact the situation of China in the forties made it impossible for later poets to adopt such a simplistic view. The group of Chinese modernist poets who came after this eventually turned to a new kind of poetry that did not aim at showing urban scenes, but tried to understand and evaluate modernity in all its complexities.

2. Literary and Socio-cultural Background of the Modernists

After *Les Contemporains* ceased publication in 1935, there appeared ephemerally on the scene in Shanghai various small poetry journals such as *Xiandai shifeng* [*Modern Trends in Poetry*] edited by Dai Wangshu, *Dangjin wenyi* [*Literature Today*], *Caihua* [*Vegetable Blossoms*] and *Shizhi* [*Poetry Gazette*] edited by Lu Yisi, as well as *Xiaoya* [*Hymns*] edited by Wu Benxing. And Bian Zhilin in Beijing had edited a literary journal *Shui xing* [*Mercury*] (1934–1935). But one important journal that combined these various efforts and initiated new trends was the poetry journal *Xinshi* which was founded in 1936 and edited by a group of prominent poets: Dai Wangshu, Bian Zhilin, Sun Dayu, Liang Zongdai, and Feng Zhi . The editors made a good selection of poems of better quality than the works in previous poetry journals. They were devoted translators who produced better translations of European poets with special sections on Jules Supervielle (Vol. I, No. 1), Pedro Salinas (Vol. I, No. 2), and William Blake (Vol. I, No. 3), Alexander Puskin (Vol. I, No. 5), A.E. Housman (Vol. I, No. 5), Manuel Altolaguirre (Vol. I, No. 6). In comparison to *Les Contemporains*, *Xinshi*, as a poetry journal, focused more on poetry and poetry criticisms. It published reviews of books of poetry regularly and correspondences between poets and critics about poetics, such as the exchange between Dai Wangshu and Lin Geng on poetic form (Vol. I, No. 1) and the discussion between Zhu Guangqian and Luo Niansheng on the issue of rhythm in Chinese poetry (Vol. I, No. 4 & No. 5).

Although regrettably the journal was closed down at the outbreak of the war, it had provided the ideal substratum for new talents to develop. Poets such as Xin Di, Wu Xinghua, Su Jinsan, who matured in the forties, first attracted public attention in the pages of *Xinshi*. And some of the prominent poets and editors continued to assert influence. Feng Zhi and Bian Zhilin taught at Southwest Associated University in wartime Kunming and helped to breed a new generation of poets. Dai Wangshu continued with his work in Hong Kong as literary editor and translator.

During the period of the Sino-Japanese War, China was in an intensely combative mood, and the anti-Japanese sentiment was high. The literature at that time, especially in the genre of war poetry, reflected the general atmosphere. Because of the Japanese occupation of main cultural centers such as Beijing and Shanghai after 1938, writers fled to interior cities, such as Gueilin, Kunming, Chongqing, and Yenan, or outlying islands such as Hong Kong, and established new cultural centers with new journals and publishing houses, and set up new trends.

Poets Ai Qing, He Qifang, and Tian Jian, like many other intellectuals and students, went to Yenan, the center of the Chinese Communist party, where guerrillas were fighting with the Japanese troops, and wrote poems of greater political concern. It was in Yenan that Mao Zedong in 1942 gave the "Talks at the Yenan Forum on Literature and Art" which laid down the basic principles of the Chinese Communist literary doctrine. Mao's talks were critical responses to the intellectuals at Yenan, emphasizing the necessity for political demands to prevail over artistic consideration. Mao strongly stressed party spirit and national character. He emphasized the class character of art and literature, and denied the existence of human nature above class. Mao's objective at that time was to use literature to serve the workers, peasants and soldiers from whom intellectuals would learn to remold themselves.[11] Following these guidelines, poetry in Yenan usually took on the form of oral poetry or street poetry, mostly written in praise of workers and peasants, or biting satires and political slogans condemning the enemy.

The literary doctrines of Yenan was also spread to the Northwestern part of China, especially in provinces such as Shanxi and Hebei. One well-known poetry group from that area, *Zhandi she* [Battlefield Association], for example, was actually formed by the Northwest Battlefield Service Group, a group sent from Yenan in 1938 to the North-western areas. The group had Tian Jian as the central figure and founded the poetry journal *Shijianshe* [Poetry Construction]. The poetry from these areas was later known as the "Jin Cha Ji School" [The Northwestern School], which closely followed the Yenan doctrines to serve the party and disseminate political ideas.[12]

Another group that expressed political concern yet retained a certain degree of independence was the "Qiyuepai" [July School]. The name came from a journal *Qiyue* [July] founded by the renowned critic Hu Feng in 1937 in Shanghai. During wartime, it was moved to Wuhan and publication continued until 1941. It was a literary magazine of mixed content which attracted a group of poets around it. At its later stage, it was loosely associated with the poetry journals *Shikendi* [Poetry Cultivation] in Chongqing and *Pingyuan congkan* [Plain Journal] in Chengdu. Hu Feng in 1942 edited a series called the *Qiyue shicong* [July Poetry Series] which included books of poems by Hu Feng, Ai Qing, Tian Jian, Sun Tian, A Long, Lu Li, Tian Lan, Ji Fang, Lu Yuan, and Zhou Difan. They thus formed a group known as the *Qiyue shipai* [July Poetry Group].[13] Hu Feng as a critic advocated a kind of poetry that stressed subjective lyricism against the objective world.

III. Literary Modernity in Chinese Poetry

Among the poets published in the series were Ai Qing and Tian Jian, as well as some of the younger poets who were influenced by Ai Qing's passion for social concern. Yet the series also included works by poet Lu Yuan whose poetry ranged from utopian fairy tales to bitter satires with the kind of complexities congenial to modernist poetry.

Another important yet different center for poetry was in Kunming. Because normal academic teaching was interrupted by the Japanese invasion, the major universities in Beijing moved to Kunming and formed *Xinan Lianda* [The Southwest Associated University] in 1938. The renowned poet Wen Yiduo was among the faculty members who retreated from Beijing to Changsha and from Changsha joined his students to walk ten thousand miles to Kunming. This long trip of sixty-eight days, and the lively atmosphere in the new campuses, opened a new phase of life for Wen and other intellectuals.[14] Wen was but one of the many poets who went to teach at the Southwest Associated University. Others were Zhu Ziqing, Feng Zhi, Shen Congwen, Yang Zhensheng, Qian Zhungshu, and among the younger generation, Bian Zhilin, Li Guangtian, and Wang Zuoliang. The famous critic William Empson also taught there during 1938–1939, and his course on Contemporary English Poetry was well received by students of literature.[15] Influenced by the ambience of Southwest Associated University, there emerged among the students a group of poets like Zheng Min, Mu Dan, Du Yunxie, and Yuan Kejia, who eventually established themselves either as poets or critics in the mid-forties. There was no obvious antagonism between the Yenan group and the Kunming group. Bian visited Yenan from 1938 to 1939, lived with the army and taught at Lu Xun Arts Institute before he went to Kunming and served as a link between Yenan and Kunming.[16] Other poets in Yenan such as Ai Qing and He Qifang were greatly admired by the young poets in Kunming.[17]

Literary groups at Southwest Associated University were very active at that time. Besides lectures, conferences, and seminars offered by the University, there were various literary societies formed by the students and faculty. *Wenyi xinbao* [*New Literary Journal*] was published in 1945. Li Guangtian and Yang Shengsheng co-edited *Shijie wenxue jikan* [*World Literature Quarterly*]. There were all sorts of literary activities, literary wall-journals, and literary societies.[18] One of the young poets and critics studying at Southwest Associated University, Wang Zuoliang, had written a good sketch of the poets in Southwest Associated University and their interest in World literature:

> The library was even smaller in the early years of the war, but the few books it had, especially the precious new books from abroad, had been devoured with the hunger and consequent lack of table manners of a Dr. Johnson. There they still lie—dog-eared, crumpled all over, often with the title-pages gone. But the young poets of Lianda [Southwest Associated University] have not read their Eliot and Auden in vain. Perhaps the Western world will find its own ignorance of the cultural East shocking when the truth is told of how, with what gusto and what dreamy eyes, these two poets are being read in distant China.[19]

The appropriation of Anglo-American poetry, the comparative perspective which led to a more sophisticated understanding of the relationship between culture and politics, distinguished the Kunming group from the poets in Yenan or other places. Their own responses to that particular war-time situation in China can be considered among the most mature and complex achievements in the history of Chinese New Poetry. Some of their important poems and criticisms which showed this trace were either written or published in Kunming around that time: Bian Zhilin's *Weilao xinji* [*Letters of Consolation*], Feng Zhi's *Shisihang* [*Sonnets*], Li Guangtian's *Shidi yishu* [*Art of Poetry*], Mu Dan's *Tanxiandui* [*Expedition*], Zhu Ziqing's *Xinshi zahua* [*Miscellaneous Talks on Poetry*].[20]

The development of modernist poetry continued after the war when some of the poets returned to Beijing and Shanghai. They published in *Wenxue zazhi* [*Literary Journal*], *Wenyi fuxing* [*Literary Renaissance*], and the literary supplement of *Dagong bao* [*Dagong Daily*]. Young poets in Beijing and Shanghai founded the two most important poetry journals *Shi Chuangzao* [*Poetry Creation*] (1947–1948) and *Zhongguo xinshi* [*Chinese New Poetry*] (1948). Their publishing house *Xingqun* [*Constellation*] also published volumes of poetry and criticism by young poets and critics—until the Nationalist Government closed it down in 1948. Their work met the same fate of rejection and indifference after the Communist Government took over in 1949. It was only after thirty years that the works of nine prominent poets from this group was published in an anthology known as *Jiuye ji* [*Nine Leaves*], including the works by Xin Di, Chen Jingrong, Hang Yuehe, Yuan Kejia, Mu Dan, Zheng Min, Du Yunxie, Tang Shi and Tang Qi.[21] And the nine poets are known since as the "Group of the Nine Leaves."

3. Aesthetic Modernity and Practical Modernity

One specific feature of the poetry written by the poets from Kunming in the forties is that they do not attempt to portray modern life as advocated in the editorial of the early magazine *Les Contemporains*. Poggioli had warned us against the kind of modernism which is only a "snobbist variant of romantic 'local color' of modern life."[22] An example which we sometimes find in the pages of *Les Contemporains*, like "Duhuidi manyue" [Full Moon of the Metropolis] by Xu Chi that comes close to the editor's idea of modern poetry, is tinged with "local color" of modern life:

> Written in Roman Numerals
> The Twelve stars represented by I, II, III, IV, V, VI, VII, VIII, IX,
>   X, XI, XII;
> Surrounding a clogwheel.
>
> Nights of full moon, the cubist and planar machines.
> The full moon that attaches to the tower of the skyscraper.
> The full moon of the metropolis under another stooping sky
>   scraper.[23]

In the first two stanzas, we find terms with modern flavor like "Roman Numerals," "clogwheel," "machine," "skyscrapers," indicating the new age of machinery. The adjectives, such as "cubist, planar," are rational and objective, not personal nor subjective. While it escapes from easy sentimentalism, it does not attempt to dig beneath the surface. The objects are described in their positions without suggesting more reflective perspectives. The full moon is situated between the skyscrapers to show the technically advanced aspects of a metropolis. The poem is in irregular lines, and the poet actually puts in the twelve Roman numerals to give the poem a superficial foreign flavor of modern life.

When we turn to a poem of the forties, Mu Dan's "May" (1940) for example, we can see that the vision is entirely different. In the poem, a stanza with traditional love themes in classical poetic form of four seven-character lines is juxtaposed to a vernacular stanza of totally different content:

> The heartless lad and the loving maid
> By the lotus pond, pledged their tie
> Now leaning on the railing alone
> She sees fluttering petals all over the sky.

> But the evening of May is vague
> After the parade of the torch and the shouting,
> No one would see,
> Those streets full of grandiose compliments pouring out
> After the talk in the newspapers of helping the poor
> No one would see,
> Those foolish people plunge into the mud,
> And the murderers, singing triumphantly of the Freedom of May
> Hold fast the main switch of all the unseen electricity[24]

Though modern terms like "the main switch of electricity" appear, they are not used to describe progression of the "local color" of modern life, but to serve as a sharp criticism of the unseen power engulfing all the common people. The juxtaposition of the regulated classical form and the vernacular free verse enhances the contrast. The stock images in the banal love song contrast sharply with the vernacular language and its syntax which, though less lyrical, enable the poet to relate to broader issues. While the language in classical Chinese poetry is usually more condensed and suggestive, the vernacular language enjoys greater freedom in including among other things abstract adjectives of four or five characters, such as "beigongweidi jiedao" [the streets full of grandiose compliments] and "jiujiminshengdi tanhua" [the talk of helping the poor], which mix together the metaphysical and the physical. The satire is particularly sharp with specific references and there are flexible spaces for further imagination in its humor and paradoxes. The month of May in classical Chinese poetry is usually linked with love, flowers, etc., while in the modern era, May reminds one of the May 4th Movement in 1919, and May 30th Event that led to the National Strike in 1925.

In these lines, the distrust of the authorities (those who "Hold fast the main switch of all the unseen electricity") is obvious. Certain inflated terms lose their meaning. The contrast is between what is seen and what is unseen, the on-stage performance and off-stage manipulation. There is a sharp critical sense in the poem. That Mu Dan's poem is different from a modern poem like "Full Moon of the Metropolis" by Xu Chi can be further illustrated by Calinescu's discussion of the two modernities: aesthetic modernity and practical modernity. Practical modernity, in Calinescu's words, is confidence in science, technology, progress, "the cult of reason, and the ideal of freedom defined within the framework of an abstract humanism, . . . the orientation toward pragmatism and the cult of action and success."[25] Aesthetic modernity is the rejection of practical modernity. In Mu Dan's poem, the words "freedom of May" are flanked between the term "murderers" and the manipulative action: "hold fast the main switch of all the unseen electricity," hence putting the word "freedom" into question. He wants to ask under what conditions freedom is handed to the people. He uses lively terminology but does not stop at showing its irony. He does not take the words at face value but reflects upon the way people manipulate the words.

Calinescu defines aesthetic modernity as a crisis concept:

> Aesthetic modernity should be understood as a crisis concept involved in a threefold dialectical opposition to tradition, to the modernity of bourgeois civilization (with its ideals of rationality, utility, progress), and, finally, to itself, insofar as it perceives itself as a new tradition of form of authority.[26]

In Mu Dan's poem, the juxtaposition of the vernacular passage and the classical one reveals an opposition to traditional values as well as poetic forms. The poem is ironic toward its own culture, which shows discrepancies between facts and names; its form also suggests doubts that any poem is a fixed form with self-contained autonomy.

4. Modernist Criticism in the Thirties and Forties

The modernist concern for self-reflection is seen in the emergence of more sophisticated criticism of poetry in the thirties and forties. It can be found in the work of such predecessors as Zhu Ziqing, Li Guangtian, Liu Xiwei, as well as in the works of such younger critics as Yuan Kejia and Tang Shi, who all share certain similarities in their criticism. They are in favor of the art of poetry, and are against the looseness and coarseness that predominates in the political poetry of the time. Li Guangtian, Liu Xiwei, as well as Tang Shi, have written extensively on their contemporaries, on such modernist poets as Bian Zhilin, Feng Zhi, as well as Zheng Min and Xin Di. Zhu Ziqing and Yuan Kejia are representative examples of critics from two generations who examine the general attitudes toward literature, and introduce Western thoughts as a means of changing the conventional attitude of criticism.

a. Zhu Ziqing

The social situation in China, both during the war in the early forties and in the post-war period of political and economical instability that lasted until the end of the forties, created much confusion, doubt and disillusionment for the general public which could not be dealt with satisfactorily by either the didactic or sentimental literature prevalent after the May 4th Movement. This was one of the reasons why some poets turned to Western modernist poetry and criticism for a discourse sufficiently self-ironic. An example of how the Chinese poets and critics turned to Anglo-American literary criticism for a new way to ruminate upon their own particular situation might be shown in the following study:

Zhu Ziqing, the renowned writer among the first generation of New Poets and editor of the poetry section of *Zhongguo xinwenxue daxi* [*Compendium of Modern Chinese Literature*] was a well-known scholar in classical literature who had a deep interest in modern literature. While he was teaching in Kunming in the forties, he translated the article "Poetry and Public World" by Archibald MacLeish into Chinese. He later included this translation in his own collection of critical essays on New Poetry, mentioned it in his collection of critical essays on New Poetry and also in another of his articles on poetry,[27] thus giving it a particular significance, not solely as a translation, but as an expression of his own idea of poetry as well.

The article "Poetry and the Public World" focuses on the merging of the public and private worlds, on how modern poets recognize the trends of the time, and on the need of a language to accommodate this. These concerns were right at the heart of the issues that intrigued Zhu and the other poets in the forties. MacLeish writes from the perspective of a modern Western writer who senses the blurring of the line between the public and the private worlds:

> If our life as members of society, which is to say our public life, which is to say our political life, has become a life which moves us to personal indignation, which fills us with personal fear, which also suggests to us private hopes, we have no choice but to say that our experiences of this life are experiences of intense and personal emotions. And if our experiences of this life are experiences of intense and personal emotions, then they are experiences that poetry can make recognizable.[28]

What concerns MacLeish, as well as Zhu, is how to present to the reader "in the personal and yet universal terms of poetry, our generation's experience of the political world" and how to organize the "public yet private life of our time" into poetry.[29]

This is the main focus of Zhu's articles on New Poetry at that time. In his article "Interpretation of Poetry," he defends ambiguity;[30] in "Poetry and Sentiment," he advocates a kind of poetry derived from acute sensitivity to simple daily life;[31] in "Poetry and Philosophy," he looks at Feng Zhi's sonnets and their ability to arrive at philosophical meditation from a daily situation;[32] in "Poetry and Humor," he examines the reason behind the observation that there is not much humor in the new literature and reflects on a common attitude which looks at poetry in an over-serious way, hence narrowing its scope.[33] In this group of articles, Zhu, citing the works of Feng Zhi, Bian Zhilin and Wen Yiduo, is defending the art of poetry, the craft of language, and the possibility for daily objects and events to enter into poetry. In another series of articles, he focuses on the dominant war poems, oral ballads, epics, and patriotic poetry of his time. He is sympathetic to these genres and understands the reason for their growth, but he also tries to speculate on a more mature and condensed way of portraying general experience. In "War and Poetry," he observes the prosaic tendency in war poems,[34] and examines the possibility of a new kind of epic in China in "Poetry and the Building of the Nation."[35] In "Patriotic Poetry," he inspects the more "modern" concept of "Nation," as expressed in Wen Yiduo's poems, which transcends one dynasty or one government.[36] From these two groups of articles, we can see Zhu arguing for a mutually respected coexistence of the personal and public type of poetry.

The term "modern" often takes on a honorific sense in Zhu's discussion, and helps to serve as a way to balance the two trends of poetry. In "Poetry and the Building of the Nation," he says:

> We need poetry that promises the modernization of China, poetry that sings of modernization, expresses the modernization of our life in general... But on the other hand, we also need the modernization of Chinese poetry, of New Poetry. Modernization will make New Poetry richer and more fertile.[37]

The term "modern" is also used to argue against the crude use of monotonous narration in oral poetry. He thinks that it may not be very fruitful for New Poetry to imitate the form of folk songs, because "Our New Poetry has already transcended these prototypes. That is because we have already accepted the foreign influence and learned to catch up with it. This is Westernization, but we better call it modernization... Modernization is inevitable."[38] In another article, he reflects upon the reason why experiments of using the folk song form for poetry since the war have not been successful: "This shows that the simple music [of folk songs] is no longer in tune with modern man's complicated feelings and thoughts."[39] And in another article he writes: "But modern life and foreign influences sharpen our sensitivity; we especially know that poetry is compressed with meaning, not only meant to be tuneful."[40]

In the article "Poetry and the Public World," Zhu sees the possibility of combining the two modes, of organizing "the public yet private life of our time" in poetry, and how to write about the public world not at the expense of the private, nor of poetry. MacLeish wrote from the position of a second-generation modernist. He was dissatisfied with early modern poetry which in his view was "a needed and cleansing poetry of literary revolt," but not "a poetry capable of the new labor of construction which must be done now." MacLeish regards this as the reason for the failure of contemporary poetry "to make recognizable to us our experiences of our time." He says: "To write in faith and credit of such experiences as ours, and to bring it to recognition requires the responsible and dangerous language of acceptance and belief."[41] This is not only the ideal of MacLeish, but the hope of the poets of China in the forties. Zhu quoted this sentence in his article "Trends of Poetry" where he reviewed an anthology of English poetry during the war: *Fear No More*. The review of the book, with its emphasis on writing about the experiences of the times, the self-conscious reflection, unadorned diction, and daily life as the subject matter of poetry, clearly reveals Zhu's expectations for Chinese poetry. The last paragraph is most obvious in stating his ideas in appropriating these trends in English poetry as models for Chinese poets:

> Our nation is now in the same war, and on the same front as these English poets. In our country, poetry since the outbreak of the Sino-Japanese War seems to have leaned toward the sentiments of the public and neglected the sentiments of the individual. There are naturally traces of over-prosaic tendencies in poetry. The anthology *Fear No More* may serve as a very good alternative for our poetry.[42]

Zhu, though in search of a way to write about contemporary experience, was also critical of the over-prosaic tendencies of the war poems of that period. His introduction to the MacLeish article was to serve this purpose—to urge a balance between public and private worlds. Zhu not only had great influence on the younger generation in Kunming where he served as a professor in Chinese literature at Southwest Associated University, but his ideas aroused echoes even in the generation after the war. In 1948, in a special issue in *Zhongguo xinshi* commemorating his death, a young critic Chen Lo wrote an article on Zhu's book of criticism, "Peixian xiansheng di xinshi zahua" [Mr. Zhu's Miscellaneous Talks on Poetry], with emphasis on Zhu's ideas on the art of poetry. In regard to MacLeish's article, the young critic, though more sympathetic to Eliot and other modernists, considered Zhu's translation of the article as an introduction to a new direction for modern poetry in China.[43] So MacLeish's idea of bringing public and private life together in poetry still serves as a reference for the younger generation.

b. Yuan Kejia

Yuan Kejia was among the group of poets who had a baptism of modernism in Southwest Associated University. He continued to write poems and criticism in Beijing after the war, and became the most influential critic of the younger generation. Understanding how his interest in Anglo-American poetry developed and what his theoretical preferences were can help us discern the characteristics of this group of modernists in the forties.

Yuan enrolled in Southwest Associated University in 1941.[44] He began his contact with Western modernism in his second year when Robert Payne offered a course in modern Anglo-American poetry and Bian Zhilin taught modern fiction with special focus on narrative perspectives. There already existed in Southwest Associated University enthusiastic literary groups with different political tendencies, as well as a general interest in modern literature. Yuan and several others started a magazine *Geng yun* [*Farming*]. The works of the young poets were also published in a small newspaper named *Shenghuo zhoukan* [*Life Weekly*], and later in *Dagong bao*. He was engaged in literary activities for four years. One of Yuan's early poems was sent to *Dagong bao* for publication by his teacher Feng Zhi who taught a course on Goethe at Southwest Associated University,[45] but Yuan did not publish much creative work in his university days. He wrote his graduation thesis on modern English and American poetry, and after his return to Beijing at the end of the war, he began to publish more poetry and a series of critical essays that stirred up a renewed interest in modernism among his peers.

In one of Yuan's articles published in *Wenxua zazhi*, "Shi di mixin" [Superstitious Attitudes toward Poetry], there is a subtitle indicting that this is a chapter from a book called *Xin piping* [*New Criticism*].[46] Yuan had actually written a ten-chapter manuscript that had over one hundred thousand words to be published under that title, but the manuscript was lost during wartime. From the published article, we can see Yuan's interest in New Criticism and Western modernism, and also his efforts to make it applicable to the criticism of Chinese literature at that time. Yuan is against certain misconceptions of literature, one of which is the belief that unrestrained emotions equal poetry:

> There is a great difference between the emotions that the poet has in the conceiving of a poem, and its final expression in the finished work. The most common procedure is: it emerges from the simple to the complex, from the institution of single points to three-dimensional structures, from the suspension of drifting, vague sentiments to vivid and accurate depiction, from the simple cell of passion, through critical examination, selection, synthesis and arrangement, to the development of a smooth, solid and profound organic structure. The empathy aroused in the readers is a long way from the original starting point of the poem. Even the poet himself would find the finished work very much different from his original notions.[47]

On the surface, Yuan would seem to have merely introduced the ideas of New Criticism from the West, yet his criticisms were always intended to change the native temperament. In one essay he would anthologize all the main ideas of the New Critics, yet subtly he is showing them as alternatives to the dominant trend. He quotes from F. A. Pottle the view on "felt belief" to dispute the uncritical acceptance of belief, and from T. S. Eliot the idea that belief has to come from concrete and mature experiences in order to thwart the emphasis on abstraction. He introduces Kenneth Burke's concept that poetry is a mode of symbolic action, R. P. Blackmur's idea of "language as gesture," Cleanth Brooks' language of paradox," and I. A. Richards's idea that poetry is the unification of opposite impulses. Yuan uses what he learned from the New Critics to react against the two main trends of poetry at that time: the sentimental and the didactic. Whether their emphasis is on love or politics, their common fault, according to Yuan, is that they have blind faith in emotion, believing that poetry will flow incessantly from the pen onto the pages once the emotions are "switched on." What Yuan calls the "superstitious attitudes" include also those blind convictions that poetry is a form of belief, that it can lead to direct action, that it is merely spoken dialect or the daily prosaic language. For Yuan, if poetry is a form of belief, it has to be felt, and to be able to arrive at maturity. Yuan believes that poetry is not the sheer recording of spoken words; its language has to be condensed and worked on. While spoken dialect may be rich and flexible, it can also create confusion among people from different provinces.[48] Yuan sees the primary duty of critics to be the advocacy of a self-conscious, rational and critical attitude toward creative writing.[49] In general, Yuan's criticism aims at the predominant ills of Chinese literature of his time. For him, one of the ways to react against the over-emotional expression and bland depiction in poetry is its modernization, and he wrote three articles calling for the modernization of New Poetry in China.[50] In his call for the modernization of poetry, one of the key terms Yuan uses is "the dramatization of poetry," a process of transferring the intellect and emotions into poetic experiences.[51] He sees the two voices he criticizes, the didactic and the sentimental, to be caused by the absence of this process of transmutation.

For the dramatization of poetry, Yuan suggests a technique like using objective correlatives in the place of direct statements. He proposes poetic drama, or internal dramatization, the coalescence of internal emotions with the surrounding environment as shown by R.M. Rilke. Another method is external dramatization. Yuan gives Auden's "The Novelists" as an example and examines Auden's method of external dramatization:

> His usual method is to depict the subject through psychological understanding, employing his wit and intellect as a poet, or his special ability of manipulating language to give it life. The poet reveals his sympathy, hate, never through plain statements.[52]

Yuan admires Auden for his insights, his diverse themes, warmth and wit. From his praises of Auden, we can see what he has learned from Auden and other modernist poets, and what he wants to achieve in the modernization of Chinese poetry. This is shown in his criticism as well as in his own poetry.

III. Literary Modernity in Chinese Poetry

5. Translation and Poetics

The Chinese modernist poets, in their search for new idioms of expression to respond to a particular socio-cultural context, sometimes learned from classical Chinese poetry and renewed the traditional mode of expression. Yet more often, they translated works from their Western counterparts as references, examples or explanations of their own methods of creation. Short introductions to translations could be read as manifestoes whereas translations of these poets were usually demonstrations of their own poetics. The translation of Western modern poetry in the forties went in a different direction from that of *Les Contemporains* in the early thirties. The works of Dai Wangshu, a poet who was active in both periods, are a good example.

Though Dai Wangshu's poems published in *Les Contemporains* still showed traces of his early period and revealed the influences of Tang poetry and Sung lyrics that had for many years given him the name of a sentimental lyrical poet, in the late thirties and the forties his poetry and his translations of French and Spanish poetry eventually established him as a major voice in Chinese modernist poetry. His earliest attempt at translation was of the English poet Ernest Dowson; then in the forties, he turned to Charles Baudelaire's *Fleur du Mal* and Federico Garcia Lorca's Ballads. Other poets from France and Spain Dai translated in this period were Victor Hugo, Remy de Gourmont, Paul Fort, Francis Jammes, Pierre Reverdy, Paul Valéry, Paul Eluard, Guillaume Apollinaire, Jules Supervielle, as well as Pedro Salinas, Rafael Alberti and Manuel Altolaguirre. When one reads through the selection of Dai's translation of poems, *Dai Wangshu yishiji* [Poetry Translations by Dai Wangshu],[53] one discovers his taste in his choice of materials and his developed interest in and sensitivity towards modern poetry. His translations are particularly revealing when read side by side with Dai's own creative works. The shift of his interest from Ernest Dowson to French and Spanish modernist poetry is parallel in many ways to the development of his poems from sentimental and nostalgic laments to a more mature and well controlled expression.

Another poet who translated French poetry is Liang Zongdai who also was one of the editors of *Xinshi*. He introduced modern French poetry into China with his two volumes of criticism, *Shi yu zhen, Shi yu zhen er ji* [Poetry and Truth, Vol. 1 & 2] and two anthologies of translations, including works by Johann Wolfgang von Goethe, William Blake, Percy Bysshe Shelley, Victor Hugo, Charles Baudelaire, Friedrich Nietzsche, Paul Verlaine, Rainer Maria Rilke and Rabindranath Tagore.[54] He is an expert on Valéry, with whom he was acquainted during his stay in France, and whose work he translated in the twenties. Valéry also wrote the preface for Liang's translation of Tao Yuanming's poems into French.[55] Liang eventually devoted more efforts to literary studies in classical and Western literature and less to creative writing.

Bian Zhilin's early translations of poems and prose by European writers, including prose poems by Charles Baudelaire, Stéphane Mallarmé, Paul Valery and Rainer Maria Rilke, were collected in *Xichuangji* [*Window to the West*]. Later selections of his works are compiled in *Yingguo shixuan* [*Translations of English Poetry*] which includes translations of poems by W. B. Yeats, T. S. Eliot and W. H. Auden, who greatly influenced him.[56] Bian is a consistent and meticulous translator. In his introduction to the translation of Auden's sonnets, he gave his criterion by which translations should: "not only be faithful to the content, but also faithful to the form." He therefore tried to work out a sonnet rhyme scheme in Chinese that could match Auden's,[57] Hence Bian's translation of Auden's sonnets indicates his concern with modernistic complexities of perspective as well as formal considerations.

During his trip to China in 1938, Auden read Sonnet XVII from the sonnet sequence "In Time of War" at a tea party where he met with the Chinese intellectuals in Hankow. The poem was translated and reprinted in the daily newspaper *Dangong bao* the following morning. Much to the surprise of Auden, the second line: "Abandoned by his general and his lice," was translated into "Qiongren yu furen lianhe qilai kangzhan [The poor and rich combine forces to fight].[58] The translation had turned the unstereotyped and realistic image of the original poem into a stereotyped slogan to prevent a sense of blasphemy that might seem unacceptable to the public. This is an illustration of the gap between the modernist vision and the prevalent Chinese treatment of the same subjects.

The poet Bian Zhilin later wrote in the article "Dushi yu xieshi" [Reading and Writing Poetry] his reflections upon this case of

III. Literary Modernity in Chinese Poetry

distortion in the translation which are indicative of the Chinese modernist's stand:

> From the viewpoint of the translator, maybe he thought: How could a Chinese general abandon his soldier? How could the word "lice" be put into a poem? Actually the poem presents a noble vision, and there is compassion between the lines. The problem is that our general readers always expect the poet to tell them explicitly that he is "sad" or "angry," otherwise they are not able to feel the emotions nor to read the poem constructively.[59]

In "Reading and Writing Poetry," Bian also criticizes the general acceptance of elaborate and pompous expressions, sentimental emotions, and stock presentations, while calling for creativity and originality. He observes that the writers of war poems in China, instead of looking around, just "stare blankly into the sky as they write."[60] In the place of abstract vocabulary and empty slogans such as "Yellow River! Tai Mountain!" he thinks poets should start with more manageable topics and more specific points.[61]

Bian was actually an admirer of Auden and a more faithful translator of five of the sonnets from "In Time of War," including Sonnet XVIII.[62] Bian himself, while staying with the guerrillas in Northwest China during 1938–39, had written a group of twenty poems published in a small volume entitled *Letters of Consolation*.[63] These poems contain portraits of peasants, workers and soldiers involved in the war, and represent a new kind of war poem that is more than mere slogans and abstract generalizations. The poet's attitude towards poetry is simultaneously shown in his translations, and his discussion of translation contains his manifesto of poetics.

In their early attempts Dai Wanshu, Liang Zongdai and Bian Zhilin were among the best translators of modern European poetry. Two other important books of poetry were also translated into Chinese in 1937 and 1938: T. S. Eliot's *The Waste Land* translated by Zhao Lorui, and R. M. Rilke's *Letters to a Young Poet*, translated by Feng Zhi[64], which suggested directions for the coming generations. Rilke's poems were first translated by Feng Zhi and later by Xu Chi, Chen Jingrong, Tang Shi and Wu Xinghua.[65] Translations of T. S. Eliot's short poems and excerpts from his criticism were scattered in various journals. His "Love Song of J. Alfred Prufrock" was translated by Mu Dan, while his "Burnt Norton" was translated by Tang Shi,[66] and the translations reveal a consciousness of such issues as images, objective correlatives, paradoxes, tensions, the use of voices and the combination of the concrete and the metaphysical in modern poetry. We can also find examples of these in Chen Jingrong's "Moshengdi cheng" [Alien City] and "Luojibingzhedi chuntian" [Spring of the Logic-maniac]; in Tang Shi's "Saodongdi cheng" [The Tumultuous City]; in Hang Yuehe's "Fuhuodi tudi" [The Rejuvenated Earth]; as well as in Tang Qi's "Shijian yu qi" [Time and the Banner]. The latter two works show the obvious influence of T. S. Eliot. But whereas one can trace parallel lines between Eliot's "Burnt Norton" and "Time and the Banner," a different concept of time is revealed in the Chinese poem through the modernist juxtaposition of images and indeterminacy of meanings. There are also more definite signals of referential meanings: the Westernized Shanghai in the late forties with mixed social strata, a Chinese land partially ceded to foreign poets, and therefore at the same time a place both Chinese and foreign, where the archaic and the modern, hope and despair, co-existed.

In the more private mode of poetry, the lyric, the poets learned their lesson from Rilke on meditation and condensation. Yet at the same time, they were conscious of the threatening forces of the public world. Hence the lyric is used as a negation of public belief, rather than as a solipsistic self-reflection. The particular qualities of the Chinese language provide constraints as well as advantages for the Chinese modernists. From poets with obvious Western links like Mu Dan, or from poets such as Wu Xinghua and Xin Di who have developed under the strong influence of classical poetry, we find in poems like "Wo" (Mu Dan), "Tan pipadi furen" [Woman Playing on the Pipa] (Wu Xinghua), and "Dujuanhua he niao" [Azalea and Cuckoo], examples of a manipulation of the particular quality of the Chinese language to arrive at modernity in Chinese poetry.

Endnotes

1. The present study is a revised version of a chapter from my doctoral dissertation, "Aesthetics of Opposition: A Study of the Modernist Generation of Chinese Poets, 1936–1949," submitted in 1984 to the

University of California, San Diego. I would like to take this opportunity to thank Professor Roy Harvey Pearce, Professor Donald Wesling, Professor Michael Davidson and especially Professor Wai-lim Yip for their thought-provoking comments and encouragement.

2. See Shi Zhecun, "Xiandai zayi" [Memories of *Xiandai*] in *Xinwenxue shiliao* [Historical Materials of Modern Literature] 1 (1981):213–220.
3. See the special issue in *Xiandai* [*Les Contemporains*] 5.6 (1934).
4. Zhi Zhecun, "Zhijiage shiren Sangdebao" [Chicago Poet Carl Sandburg], *Xiandai* 3.1 (1933):117.
5. Shao Xunmei, "Xiandai meiguoshi gaikuang" [Panoramic View of Modern American Poetry], *Xiandai* 5.6 (1934):878–886.
6. Shi Zhecun, "Youguanyu benkandi shi" [More About the Poems in this Magazine], *Xiandai* 4.1 (1934):6–7.
7. Ibid., 7
8. See for example, the Introduction to *Xiandai Zhongguo shixuan* [*Modern Chinese Poetry: An Anthology, 1917–1949*], ed. M.M.Y. Fung et al. (Hong Kong: Hong Kong University Press and the Chinese University of Hong Kong Publication Office, 1974) 21.
9. Renato Poggioli, *The Theory of the Avant-Garde* [New York: Harper and Row, 1971) 128.
10. Ibid., 220.
11. Mao Zedong, *Mao Zedong xuanji* [*Selected Works of Mao Zedong*] (Beijing: Foreign Language Press, 1967) 69–98
12. See Dan Hui, "Jinchaji shige zhanxiandi yizhi qingqibing" *Xinwenxue shiliao* 4 (1981).
13. For information and works of the July Poets, see the two anthologies edited in the 1980s: Lu Yuan and Niu Han, ed., *Baise hua* [*White Flowers*] (Beijing: Renmin Wenxue 1981); and Zhou Liangpei, ed., *Qiyue* [*July*] (Chengdu: Sichuan Renmin, 1984).
14. See Kai-yu Hau, *Wen I-to* (Boston: Twayne, 1980) 135–151.
15. The information was from my interview with Yuan Kejia conducted in San Diego, California on November 16, 1980.
16. See Bian Zhilin "Zizhuan" [Autobiography], *Zhongguo Dangdai Zuojia Zizhuan* [*Autobiography of Contemporary Chinese writers*] (n.d.) rpt. Macau: Center for Modern Chinese Literature), 4–10.
17. See for example Mu Dan's review of Ai Qing's poem "Ta sizai dierci" [He Died the Second time] in *Dagong bao* [*Dagong Daily*], April 28, 1940. See also Wen Yiduo's [*The Complete Works of Wen Yiduo*, ed. Zhu Ziqing et al., (Shanghai: n.p., 1948) 223–238. His lectures on Ai Qing and Tian Jian were given in Southwest Associated University and collected in vol. 6 of *Wen Yiduo quanji* 51–53.

18. The information was obtained from my interview with Yuan Kejia.
19. Wang Zouliang, "A Chinese Poet," *Life and Letters*, June 1949: 200.
20. Bian Zhilin, *Weilaoxin ji* [Letters of Consolation] (Hong Kong: Mingri She, 1942); Feng Zhi, *Shisihang ji* [Sonnets] (Gueilin: Mingri, 1942); Li Guangtian *shidi ishu* [Art of Poetry] (Beiping: Kaiming, 1855); Mu Dan *Tanxiandui* [The Expedition] (Kunming: Chungwen, 1945); Zhu Ziqing *Xinshi Zahua* [Miscellaneous Talks on Poetry] (Beijing: Zuojia Shuwu, 1949). Bian arrived at Kunming in 1940; the works of Feng, Mu and Zhu were all written in Kunming in the early forties.
21. Yuan Kejia et al., *Jiuye Ji* [Nine Leaves] (Jiangau: Renmin, 1981).
22. Renato Poggioli, *The Theory of the Avante-Garde*, trans. Gerald Fitzgerald (New York: Harper & Row, 1971).
23. Xu Chi "Duhui de manyue [Full Moon of the Metropolis] *Xiandai* 5.1 (1934): 180.
24. Mu Dan, "Wuyue" [May], in *Mu dan Shiji* [Selected Poems of Mu Dan] (n.p.: n.p., 1947) 41–42.
25. Matei Calinescu, *Faces of Modernity: Avant Garde, Decadence, Kitsch* (Bloomington and London: Indiana University Press, 1977).
26. *Ibid*.
27. Zhu Ziqing, trans. "Shi yu gongzhong shijie" [Poetry and the Public World] by Archibald MacLeish, *Dagong bao* 8 April, 1940. The translation was collected in *Xinshi Zahua* [Miscellaneous Talks on Poetry] (1947; rpt. Hong Kong: Xinwenxue Yanjiu Zhongxin, 1963) 111–126. It was mentioned in "Shidi qushi" [Trends in Poetry] in *Xinshi zahua*.
28. Archibald MacLeish, "Poetry and the Public World," in *Atlantic Monthly*, 163.6 (1939): 827.
29. *Ibid*, 827.
30. Zhu, "Jieshi" [Interpretations of Poetry], *Xinshi zahua*, 4–8.
31. Zhu, "Shi yu ganjue [Poetry and Sentiment], *Xinshi zahua* 9–17.
32. Zhu, "Shi yu jieli [Poetry and Philosophy], *Xinshi zahua* 18–23.
33. Zhu, "Shi yu youmo" [Poetry and Humor], *Xinshi zahua* 24–33.
34. Zhu, "Zhanzheng yu shi" [War and Poetry], *Xinshi zahua* 38–45.
35. Zhu, "Shi yu jianguo" [Poetry and the Building of the Nation], *Xinshi zahua* 38–45.
36. Zhu, "Aiguo shi" [Patriotic Poetry], *Xinshi zahua* 46–53.
37. Zhu, *Xinshi zahua* 41.
38. Zhu, *Xinshi zahua* 85.
39. Zhu, *Xinshi zahua* 91.
40. Zhu, *Xinshi zahua* 107.
41. MacLeish, 829–830.
42. Zhu, *Xinshi zahua* 64–65.

43. Chen Lo "Peixian xiansheng di *Xinshi zahua*" [Miscellaneous Talks on Poetry by Mr. Zhu], *Zhongguo Xinshi* [*Chinese New Poetry*], (Sept. 1948): 10–14.
44. This and the following information are from my personal interview with Yuan Kejia.
45. Yuan, "Wo Gechangzai jinse taiyangdi bianyuanshang" [I Sing at the Edge of the Golden Dawn], *Dagong bao* 7 July, 1943.
46. Yuan, "Shidi mixin" [Superstitious Attitudes Toward Poetry], *Wenxue zazhi* [*Literary Journal*], 12.11 [1947]: 7.
47. Ibid., 9.
48. Ibid., 7–13.
49. Yuan, "Dangian pipingdi renwu" [The Immediate Duty of a Critic], *Wenxue zazhi* 2.7 (1946): 33–37.
50. The three articles are: 1. "Xinshi xiandaihua" [The Modernization of New Poetry] *Dagong bao* 30 March, 1947; 2. "Xinshi xiandaihua de fenxi" [*Analysis of the Modernization of New Poetry*], *Dagong bao*, 18 May 1947; 3. "Xinshi xijuhua" [Dramatization of Poetry], *Wenxue zazhi* 3.1 (1947), 28–31.
51. Yuan, "Xinshi xijuhua," revised and reprinted in *Shichuangzao* [*Poetry Creation*], 12 (1948).
52. *Ibid.*
53. Dai Wangshu, *Dai Wangshu Yishiji* [*Poetry Translations by Dai Wangshu*] (Hunan: Renmin, 1983).
54. For Liang Zongdai's introduction of modern French poetry, see his two volumes of criticism: *Shi yu Zhen* [*Poetry and Truth*] (Shanghai: Shangwu, 1934) and *Shi Yu zhen erji* [*Poetry and Truth, Vol. II*] (Shanghai: Shangwu, 1936). See also his two anthologies of translation: *Yiqie di fengding* [*Summit of the Universe*], ed., Chen Ying (1934; rpt. Taipei: Dadi, 1976) and *Liang Zongdai yishiji* [*Liang Zongdai's translation of Western Poetry*] (Hunan: Renmin, 1983).
55. See *Shi yu zhen* 125–134.
56. Bian Zhilin, *Xichuang ji* [*Window to the West*] (Shanghai: Shangwu, 1936); and *Yingguo shixuan* [*Translations of English Poetry*] (Hunan: Renmin, 1983).
57. Bian Zhilin, trans., "Zhanshi zaizhongguo zuo" (Five Sonnets from *In Time of War* by Auden], *Zhongguo xinshi* [*Chinese New Poetry*], July, 1948: 11–12.
58. See Bian Zhilin, "Dushi he xieshi". [Reading and Writing Poetry], *Dagong bao*, 20 Feb., 1941.
59. Bian, "Dushi he xieshi."
60. *Ibid.*

61. *Ibid.*
62. Bian's translation is in *Zhongguo xinshi* 2 (1948): 11–14.
63. Bian, *Weilaoxin ji* [*Letters of Consolation*] was first published in Hong Kong in 1940. It was collected in *Shinian shicao* [*Poetry of a Decade*] (Gueilin: Mingri, 1942) 133–195.
64. The translation of *The Waste Land* by Zhao Lorui was reprinted in *Waiguo xiandaipai zuopinxuan* [*Selections from Western Modernist Literature*], ed. Yuan Kejia, Vol. 1, Part I (Shanghai: Wen I, 1980), 88–121. Rilke's *Letters to a Young Poet* translated by Feng Zhi was first published in Kunming in 1938 and reprinted in Hong Kong by Jianwen Press in 1959.
65. We could find Feng Zhi's translation of five of Rilke's poems in *Xinshi* [*New Poetry*] 1.3 (1936): 285–293; Xu Chi translated one poem in *Shichuangzao* 10 (1984): 10–11, and seven poems in *Zhongguo xinshi* 2 (1948): 19–23. Tang Shi translated four poems which were published in *Huamei wenbao* on August 16, 18, 23 and September 30, 1948 respectively. Wu Xinghua's translation of five poems were later reprinted Taiwan's *Wenxue zazhi* [*Literary magazine*] 1.2 (1956): 6–12 and 1.4 (1957) 18–40.
66. Mu's translation of "Love Song of J. Alfred Prufrock by T. S. Eliot was reprinted in *Waiguo Xiandaipai zuopinxuan* 74–87. Tang's translation of "Burnt Norton" was published in *Shichuangzao* 10 (1948):15–19.

Feng Zhi (1905–)

From the *Sonnets of Feng Zhi*

1.

We are prepared to receive deeply
Those unforeseen miracles.
In our long months and years suddenly
Appears a comet; blasts of wind.

Our life at this instant
Seems still in its first embrace.
Past joys and sorrows all abruptly
Clot into unmovable forms.

We praise those small insects
Which after but one intercourse
Or after resisting one peril

Will end their wonderful lives.
Our entire course is to take in
Blasts of wind, appearance of a comet.

15.

Look! These caravans of horses
Brought us goods from distant provinces.
Water may carry here sand and soil
From unknown places far away.

Winds from beyond thousands of miles
Will also blow here sighs of other lands.
We pass through many mountains and rivers
At all hours occupying them, at all hours discarding them.

Like birds soaring in the sky,
At all hours commanding the space,
At all hours feeling empty and void.

What, then, is our *reality*?
From distant provinces nothing can be brought here.
From here, nothing can be taken away.

16.

We stand abreast on top of high peaks
And change into endless distant views,
Into the vast, vast plain before us,
Into crisscrossing paths and trails on it.

This road, that river, no connection.
This wind, that cloud, no correspondence.
The cities, mountains, rivers that we passed
Are changed into part of our life.

Our growth, our sorrows
Are a lone pine on such-and-such a slope,
Are thick fog across such-and-such a city:

We are blown with the wind, we flow with water
And change into paths and trails on the plain
Into the lives of travellers upon them.

18.

We often pass a night warm and intimate
In an unfamiliar room whose shape
In the daytime we have no way to know,
Let alone its past, its future. The plain

Endlessly stretches before our window.
We vaguely remember the road we came by
In the dusk: such is our knowledge.
Tomorrow, we will leave and return no more.

Close our eyes then! Let these warm, intimate nights
And unfamiliar places weave in our heart:
Our life is like the plain outside the window.

Upon the misty plain we recognize
A tree, a flash of lake-light; within the boundlessness
Is hidden the forgotten past, the seen-unseen future.

21.

We listen to raging rains in whirlwinds.
We are much too much alone by the lamp.
Inside this small small straw hut
Even between our daily appliances

Extend a million miles of distance.
Toward ores in deep mountains, brass burners.
Toward the river-clay, ceramic teapots.
They are like birds in windblown rains,

Scattering east, scattering west. We hold tight
Ourselves as if ourselves can no longer be held.
Whirlwinds blow everything into the high sky.

Raging rains rain everything into the soil,
Leaving this one mere ray of weak lamp's red
To witness the short-livedness of our life.

23.

Two weeks on end of ceaseless rain.
All you knew since your birth
Was but wetness and gloominess.

One day, rainclouds dispersed.
Your mother held you by her mouth
And took each of you into the sun
To let you, your entire body

Receive light and warmth for the first time.
She waited until sundown and
Again took you all back home. You

Had no memory, but this scene, this
Experience will blur into your future barking.
You will bark and spark light in deep night.

26.

Every day we walk on a familiar road
To return to our dwelling place;
But inside this forest are hidden still
Many small paths, deep, dark, and strange

Upon which our hearts throb
With fear of getting lost as we move further in.
And yet suddenly through the branches
We may again see our dwelling place

Like a new island emerging from the horizon.
How many things there are around us
That demand our re-discovery?

Don't think that everything is familiar.
At your death-bed, even as you stroke your hair,
You may ask: Whose body is this?

27.

From a free-flowing stretch of shapeless water
A man fetches some in an oval bottle.
This much water thus acquires a definite shape.
Look, the flags fluttering in the autumn winds

Take hold of certain things that cannot be held.
Let lights and nights from the distance,
Let ups and downs of trees and grass,
Let the desire to reach for infinity

Be preserved upon these flags.
We listen in vain to a whole night of winds
Watch in vain grass turn yellow, leaves red.

Where are we to anchor our thoughts?
I wish that these poems, like flags,
Could hold certain things that cannot be held.

Dai Wangshu (1905–1950)

The Alley in the Rain

Holding an oil-paper umbrella, alone,
I hesitate in a long, long,
Sparse, quiet alley in the rain.
Would that I encountered
A girl, sorrow-laden,
Like a lilac.

A girl with
Color like the lilac,
Fragrance like the lilac,
Sadness like the lilac,
Pensive in the rain,
Hesitating and pensive.

Hesitating in this sparse, quiet alley in the rain,
Holding an oil-paper umbrella,
Like me,
Like me,
Moving slowly, silently,
Cold, plaintive, melancholy.

She comes quietly closer,
Closer, casts
A glance like a sigh,
And floats past
Like a dream,
Like the misty grief in a dream.

Floating past like a dream,
Like a twig of lilac,
This girl floats past me,
And quietly moves away, away,
Toward the broken bamboo-fence,
And lost in the alley in the rain.

In the sad refrain of the rain,
Has disappeared her color,
Has disappeared her fragrance,
Has disappeared even her
Sigh-laden glance,
The lilaclike melancholy.

Holding an oil-paper umbrella, alone,
I hesitate in a long, long,
Sparse, quiet alley in the rain.
Would that I encountered
A girl, sorrow-laden,
Like a lilac.

From *My Memory* (1929)

Before the Ancestral Temple

Upon the dark, dark water that
Passed before the ancestral temple
Are impressed I don't know how many
Light, light footprints of my thoughts,
Lighter, swifter than those
Of the long-legged water-spiders.

From the dense green of the scholartree,
It leaps lightly to the
Water now saturated with an ancient bell's ringing,
Past ripples, over duckweeds,
Stepping with small, small,
Swift steps.

Then, hesitating,
It grows with wings . . . . . .

It flies upward,
This little madfly,
No, butterfly, flapping vigorously,
Among reeds, upon red smartweeds.
It rises higher
To become a lark
Scattering on the ground crystal voices . . . . . .
Now, it is a huge roc
Cruising among white clouds
In the vague, misty, wide skyblue.
It slowly extends its wings
To make its nine-million-mile flight,
That happy excursion* of past and future lives.

It circles around, alone,
Upon distant cloud-mountains
On the edge of the human world,
Continuously, non-stop, stubborn, almost pitiable.

Finally, in great despair,
It speeds back to my heart,
And, with anxious sorrows, crouches there.

      From Wang-shu: *Selected Poems* (1937)

---

*"Happy Excursion" is the title of the first chapter of the Daoist text *Zhuangzi* in which a flight of non-dependence on a cosmic scale is depicted.

My Memory

My memory is loyal to me,
More loyal than my best friend.

It exists in a lit cigarette.
It exists on a pen painted with lilies.
It exists in an old broken powder-box.
It exists in the wood-fungi among ruins.
It exists in a half-emptied wine bottle,
In torn drafts of poetry, on petals pressed dry,
Upon dim lamps, over still water,
Among all the things, soul or no soul.
It exists everywhere the way I exist in the world.

It is timid, abhors the hustle-bustle of people,
But in seclusion, it will pay me an intimate visit.
Its voice is low,
But it is long-winded, very long-winded,
Long, and trivial, and endless.
Its words are old; it tells the same story over and over again.
Its tune is harmonious; it sings the same song over and over again.

Sometimes it even mimics a sweet girlish voice
Which is feeble,
Mixed with tears, with sighs.

Its visits are erratic.
It may come any time, any place,
Often when I am in bed, dozing off into sleep,
Or very early in the morning.
People say that this is ill-mannered,
But we are old friends.

It will go on tediously and endlessly,
And will not stop until I cry

Or fall asleep,
But I never loathe it,
Because it is loyal to me.

1928?

Tightly-closed Garden

The garden in May
Is already flower-laden, overflowing with leaves,
But in the dense shades, all quiet, no birds' clamor.

All paths are moss-grown,
And the padlock on the bamboo-gate already rusted —
The master is in distant provinces under the sun.

Under the sun in distant provinces,
Is there a garden, equally gorgeous?

Strangers poke their heads over the bamboo-gate,
Thinking vainly of the master beyond the sky.

From Wangshu Cao (1932)

Dream-seeker

Flowers will bloom from dreams.
Charming, delicate flowers will bloom from dreams:
Go then to seek your invaluable jewels.

In the great blue sea,
At the bottom of the great blue sea,
Is hidden a gold-colored shell.

You climbed the iceberg for nine years.
You sailed the dry sea for nine years.
Then, you encountered this gold-colored shell.

It has the clouds and rains of the sky.
It has the winds and waves of the sea.
It will make your heart all drunken.

Fed by the sea-water for nine years,
Fed by the sky-water for nine years,
And then, in one dark night, it bloomed.

When your hair and sideburns turn frostwhite,
When your eyes blur with everything,
The gold-colored shell will spit out a peach pearl.

Hold the peach pearl in your bosom,
Put the peach pearl by your pillow,
A dream, thus, quietly arises.

Flowers are blooming from your dreams.
Charming, delicate flowers are blooming from your dreams,
When you are getting old, getting old.
                                        1931?

Paradiso Bird

Flying, flying, spring, summer, autumn, winter,
Day, night, to no end.
Flower-feathered paradiso bird,
Is this cloud-ride of happiness,
Or perpetual labor?

You drink dews when thirsty.
You drink dews when hungry,
Flower-feathered paradiso bird,
Is this the feast of fairies,
Or nostalgia for the celestial?

Did you come from paradise?
Or are you going there?
Flower-feathered paradiso bird,
In this vague edgeless blue sky,
Do you feel lonely in your flight?

If you are from paradise,
Can you tell us,
Flower-feathered paradiso bird
Since Adam and Eve were driven out,
How barren and waste has the celestial garden become?
                                        1931?

With My Maimed Palm

With my maimed palm,
I feel this vast land:
This corner, now ashes,
That corner, only blood and mud;
This lake must then be my home village,
(In spring, upon the dike, brocade flowers bloom;
Broken willow-twigs give forth a wonderful scent.)
I touch duckweeds and feel the coolness of water;
The snow-capped Changbai Ranges are bone-penetrating cold.
The silt-filled Yellow River slides through my fingers.
Rice paddies south of the Yangtze, new growths were once
So fine, so tender . . . . . . Now, only wild weeds:
The lichee-nut flowers of the South, all haggard and lonely.
Beyond, I dip in the bitter water of the boatless South Sea . . . . .
My invisible palm flies across endless mountains and rivers,
Fingers stained by blood and ashes, palm by darkness.
Only one distant corner remains intact,
Warm, bright, solid and alive like spring.
There, my maimed palm tenderly strokes
As one would with a lover's hair or a baby with his mother's breasts.

I put full strength in my palm
Upon that corner, placing on it love and hope,
Because it is there alone that has sun and spring
Which will drive darkness away in its rejuvenation.
Because there, we don't have to live like an animal,
Die like an ant . . . . . . There, an everlasting China.
                              1942

Ai Qing (1910–   )

Old Man

On the left side of the vertical line,
Half a tattered black uniform.
Three copper buttons along the straight edge
Flash three light yellow oil-lamps.
　—The oil is almost dried.
His purple bronze face emits some ancient light.
Within the skin of cracked palms of
Bent hands, aging roots curl up.
With it, he grips at the tail of a convulsive life.
　—A loach caught in the mud,
He rocks his ancient bronze forehead.
White froth splashes: some cursed flowers.

The color of hunger
Comes over to all his words.
                                            1933

A Prisoner in the Hospital

O hothouse for my tuberculosis!

Gauze wrapped into a hibiscus flower
Breathing with a drunken scent;
Death, wings flapping, is prowling around.
Buzzing, bees' buzzing, the Sister saying mass.

Note: Not long after the poet was arrested, he got tuberculosis and was imprisoned in the police station in the French Concession. The routine was that when someone was sick or about to die, Sisters would be sent by the church to say mass.

Thus, morning dews
Become the holy water for the dead's forehead.

Iron gates cluster like a forest of trees.
Iron gates divide us from the world.

People will say: "We all embrace
Our Christ in pain."
We stretch out two red lips
To kiss the bloody pus from our heart.

Pompeii's fire-red clouds float across my face,
The Sister sticks a thermometer
Into my volcanic mouth.

When a black cat quietly passes,
People will be busy cleaning up the bedding of the dead.

O hothouse for my tuberculosis!
Riding upon 150° temperature,
From my lilac-like lung lobes,
I spit out a depressingly beautiful flower.

                                        1934

The Mass

Electric waves whistle on the wires, in the quiet sky,
Like two hands pressing upon ten or twenty piano keys.
In my heart, too, are often dumbfounding sounds
Vying to rush out and whistle in the sky.

A drop of water often makes me stare and start at it.
Before me suddenly would appear a boundless river.
I have to merely open my mouth to find myself gasping,
As if a million people are breathing through this small hole.

When I feel with my fingers my own pulses,
My heart would be pounded by surging tides of blood.
Their pains and desires are so intertwined with mine—
When did their blood start to flow into my veins?

What is it over there—so many, so many . . . . . .
Countless feet, countless hands, countless jostling heads,
At windows, upon streets, upon piers, at stations . . . . . .
What are they doing? thinking? desiring? . . . . . .

This is a terrifying miracle: when I now remember
I am no longer myself, but a number,
Which is slowly undergoing metamorphoses, expanding
So large until I am stunned, convulsed.

When I am still, my heart is trodden over by countless feet.
When I move, my heart is like a bustling crossroad.
I sit here. On the street are countless people.
Suddenly, I see myself like a grain of dust rolling among them.

Big Weir River—My Wet Nurse

Big Weir River was my wet nurse.
Her name was the name of the village of her birth.
She was a child-bride.
Big Weir River was my wet nurse.

I was the son of a landlord.
Growing up feeding on Big Weir River's milk,
I was also the son of Big Weir River.
Raising me, Big Weir River raised her family.
I grew up feeding on your milk
You, Big Weir River, my wet nurse.

Today, I saw snow and thought of you, Big Weir River,
Of your straw tomb weighed down by snow,
Of the withered growth on eaves-tiles of your closed house,

Of the one square yard of your garden already pawned away,
Of the mossgrown stone-stool before your door.
Today, I saw snow and thought of you, Big Weir River.

You held me in your bosom with your thick palms, petting me,
After you had finished making the furnace fire,
After you had patted off ashes upon your apron,
After you had tasted that the rice was ready,
After you had placed black bowls upon the black table,
After you had patched the clothes of your sons torn by mountain thorns,
After you had bandaged your small son's hand cut by a knife while chopping wood,
After you had picked and killed the fleas on shirts of your husband and sons,
After you had picked up today's first egg,
You held me in your bosom with your thick palms, petting me.

I am the son of a landlord.
After I had finished drinking all your milk,
I was taken back to my natural parents' home.
O Big Weir River, why did you cry?

I became the new guest of my natural parents' home!
I touched the red-lacquered carved furniture;
I touched the gold patterns of my parents' bed;
I vacantly looked at the unknown "Big Family Harmony" tablet under the eaves;
I touched the silk or shell buttons of my new clothes;
I looked at my unfamiliar kid sister in my mother's bosom;
I sat on the *kang*-stool* ready with a fire bowl;
I ate white rice that had been milled three times,
But I was uneasy, fidgety! Because I
I became the new guest of my natural parents' home.

---

* In North China, this is part of a heatable brick bed.

Big Weir River, to survive,
After her flow of milk was drained,
Began to work with the arms that once held me.
Smiling, she washed our clothes.
Smiling, with shopping basket, she went to the frozen pond outside the village.
Smiling, she cut the radish like grating ice.
Smiling, she mixed wheat grains for pigs with her hand.
Smiling, she fanned the oven which was slowcooking meat.
Smiling, she carried on her back bamboo baskets to the square to sun soybeans and wheat.
Big Weir River, to survive,
After her flow of milk was drained,
Began to work with the arms that once held me.

Big Weir River loved her nursing infant deeply;
Near New Year, for him, she busied herself cutting rice candy.
For him, she often secretly went home outside the village,
So that he would walk to her side to call her "Ma".
Big Weir River, she pasted his bright red bright green
    General Guan picture upon the furnace wall.
Big Weir River, she praised loudly to her neighbors about her nursing infant
Big Weir River had a dream she could not tell others:
In that dream, she was enjoying her nursing infant's wedding party,
Sitting upon a brightly decorated hall
As her charming daughter-in-law lovingly called her "Mom"......
Big Weir river, she loved her nursing infant deeply!

Big Weir River, before awakening from her dream, she was dead.
When she died, her nursing infant was not at her side.
When she died, even her abusive husband shed tears.
Her five sons all cried with cutting grief.
When she died, she quietly called her nursing infant's name.
Big Weir River is now dead.
When she died, her nursing infant was not at her side.

Big Weir River, restraining tears, has departed!

Together with forty years of insults from the lifeworld,
Together with countless miseries of a slave,
Together with a four-dollar coffin and a few bouquets of hay,
Together with a few square feet of burial ground,
Together with a handful of ashes from burnt paper money.
Big Weir River, restraining tears, has departed!

These, however, Big Weir River did not know:
Her drunken husband is dead.
Her first son became a bandit.
Her second son died in the smoke of cannons.
Her third, fourth and fifth
Are leading lives under constant shouts from landlords and masters.
When I came back home after drifting abroad a long time,
And met them, my brothers, in the mountains, on the fields,
We are closer than six or seven years ago.
These, quietly sleeping Big Weir River,
You did not know!

Big Weir River, today, your nursing infant is in prison,
Writing a poem of praise to you,
To your purple soul under yellow earth,
To your stretched hands that once embraced me,
To your lips that once kissed me,
To your soilblack but tender face,
To your breasts that fed me,
To your sons, my brothers,
To all the wet nurses that are like my Big Weir River
And their children on this earth.
To Big Weir River who loved me the way she loved her children.

Big Weir River
I grew up feeding on your milk.
Your son
    I respect you
    I love you.

                      Snowy morning. Jan 14, 1933

Reed-Pipe

In Memory of the late G. Apollinaire

J'avais un mirliton que je n'aurais pas échange contre un baton de maréchal de France

—G. Apollinaire

I brought back from your colorful Europe
A reed-pipe.
With it,
I had walked along the Atlantic
Like walking at home.
Now,
Your *Alcools* is inside Shanghai's police station.
I am a "criminal".
Here,
The reed-pipe is also tabooed
O that reed-pipe,
It is my sincerest memory of Europe.
Mr. Apollinaire,
You are not only Polish,
Because in my eyes
You are really a legend
Circulated in Montmarte,
That longish,
    enchanting violet legend
Coming out from the trembling, rouge-fading,
Lips of Marguerite.
Who shouldn't spit
Some saliva of disdain
Upon the Empire of Briand and Bismarck —
Upon that Europe of debased robbers
Whose eyes were filled with avarice!
But,
I indulge myself in your Europe,

The Europe of Baudelaire and Rimbaud.
There,
Suffering hunger,
I blew my reed-pipe arrogantly.
People laughed at my attitude,
Because that was my attitude!
People could not get used to my song,
Because that was my song!
Off from me!
You who once sang "La Marseillaise"
Is now molesting
That which is called glory and victory!
Today,
I am in the prison of Bastille,
Not, not the Bastille of Paris.
The reed-pipe is not by my side.
Iron-shackles are louder than my song.
But I swear—as to the reed-pipe
Because its suffering from insults,
I will stretch my hand into scorching flames
Like in the explosive year of 1789.
When it comes out,
It will send out
A destructive song of curse
Upon those who humiliate its world.
And I will raise it way high,
And, with a tragically solemn Hymne,
Send it to the sea
To the sea's waves
To the savagely
Roaring waves!

March 28, 1933

Snow Falls on the Land of China

Snow falls on the land of China
Cold locks the entire nation......

Wind,
Like an old woman too sorrowful
Following closely at our heels
Stretches her cold claws
Pulling at the clothes of passers-by
And with words ancient as earth
Ceaselessly mumbles

Emerging from the woods
Hurrying horse-carts along
You, peasants of China
Wearing a leather hat
Bracing the heavy snow
Where are you going?

Let me tell you
I, too, am a descendent of peasants—
From your face
Run all over by painful wrinkles
I can tell
And deeply feel
The days & months & years of hardship
Of you folks living upon the prairies

And I
Am not happier either
—Lying on the river of Time
Surges of disasters
How many times in and out I have been thrown?
Wandering and then in prison
I have lost the heyday
Of my youth

My life
Like yours
Haggard, the same

Snow falls on the land of China
Cold locks the entire nation . . . . . .
Following the rivers of snowy night
A small oil-lamp slowly moves
The boat of torn bamboo awnings
Shines with the light
Head-hanging
Who is it sitting there?

O, you
A young woman with dishevelled hair
Is it that your home
—once nest of happiness and warmth —
Is burnt to the ground
By the brutal enemies?
Is it that
In a night like this
Having lost the protection of a man
Caught up in the terror of death
You have been insulted by the enemies?
Is it that
In a night like this
Having lost the protection of a man
Caught up in the terror of death
You have been insulted by the enemies' daggers?

Ai, it is in a night cold like this
Numerous
Aging mothers of ours
Have to crouch inside their homes
Like strangers in a strange land
Not knowing what course
Will tomorrow's wheels roll—
—And

Roads in China
Are so tortuous
And so mud-filled!

Snow falls on the land of China
Cold locks the entire nation . . . . . .

Through the prairies of the snowy night
In the regions gnawed by the fires of war
Numerous land-tillers
Have lost their fowls
Lost their fertile fields
All crowding toward
A polluted alley of hopelessness:
Hunger-stricken land
Stretches toward the darkened sky
His two begging arms
Trembling

The sufferings and disasters of China
Are wide and long like this snowy night!

Snow falls on the land of China
Cold locks the entire nation . . . . . .

China
In this unlit night
These feeble lines I have written
Can they give you a little bit of warmth?

Night, Dec. 28, 1937

The North

One Day
The poet from the steppe of Ke-er-chin
Said to me:
"The North is sorrowful."
Yes
The North is sorrowful.
The desert winds
From beyond the Pass
Have already taken away life's green in the North
As well as the light of the day
—An expanse of darkening grey-yellow
Shrouded with a sand-mist that defies lifting.
The roaring that rushes here from the sky's edge
Bringing terror,
Madly
Sweeps across the earth.
The desert plains
Freeze in the cold winds of December—
Villages, slopes, river banks,
Broken walls and deserted tombs
All have now taken on an earth-colored melancholy . . . . . .
A lone traveller
Torso bending forward,
Cupped hand shielding face,
Breathing with difficulty
In the sandstorm,
One step, another step,
Struggles to press forward . . . . . .
Several donkeys
    —with grieving eyes
    and tired-out ears
Carry the painful
Weight of the land;
Their weary steps
Sluggishly tread
Across the long long lonely road

Of the North country . . . . . .

Those small rivers are all dried.
The riverbed is full of crisscross ruts.
The land and the people of the North
Thirst for
A life-moistening fountain.
Dry, dead forest trees
And low, dwarf houses
Sparingly, gloomily,
Scatter under the grey dark sky
Where no sun
Is seen,
But a long line of wildgeese,
A turmoil of wildgeese,
Beating black wings
Crying out their anxiety and sorrow,
Fleeing from this bleak land
All the way
To the skycovering green of the South . . . . . .

The North is sorrowful,
And the Yellow River, a million miles long,
Raging with its muddy waves
Pour over the vast North
Disasters and catastrophes
And windblown frosts of centuries
Carve the vast North
Into poverty and hunger.

And I,
A traveller from the South,
Fall in love with this sorrowful North.
Face-sweeping sandstorms
And bone-penetrating cold air
Have never led me to curse it.
I love this sorrowful country.
An endless stretch of bleak desert

Would evoke my awe,
As I see
Our ancestors
Leading herds of sheep,
Playing bamboo flutes,
Immersed into the dusk of the Desert.
We tread upon
This ancient and soft loess
Beneath which are buried our ancestors' bones.
This land was cultivated by them
Several thousands of years ago.
It is here that they
Wrestled with the onslaught of nature.
To protect this land
Never once would they condescend.
Dead,
They left us this land—
I love this sorrowful country;
Its vast but barren land
Has given us a rustic simple language
And an open wide outlook.
I believe that this language and outlook
Will live on firmly on this earth,
Never to decline.
I love this sorrowful country,
    this ancient land.
It is this land
That has nourished the people I love,
The people with the hardest lives,
The oldest people of the world.

                              Tong-guan
                              Feb. 4, 1938

Beggars

In the North,
Beggars wander along the banks of the Yellow River
Or along both sides of the railroads.

In the North,
Beggars cry out their pains
With voices that most weary us,
Saying that they came from disaster areas,
From the war zone.

Hunger is to be feared.
It makes the old lose kindness,
The young turn hateful.

In the North,
Beggars stare at you
With stubborn eyes,
Looking at anything you eat
And the way you pick your teeth with fingernails.

In the North,
Beggars stretch out forever stretching hands,
Soilblack hands,
Begging for a mere coin
From anybody
From even a soldier who has not even a dime.

    Spring 1939, on way to Longhai

Bian Zhilin (1910–)

West Changan Street

Long is the slanting, slanting, faint shadows
Of dead trees, of the old man walking under the trees,
Of the cane on which he leans,
All upon the wall, the red wall of the afterglow.
Long also is the red wall, the blue sky beyond the wall,
The blue sky of the North is very long, very long.
O! Old man, this road, to you, must be
Long? The days in winter, to you, must be also
Very long? Yes, I believe.
Look! I am now closer, why not
Talk as we walk, about this, about that?
But we say nothing to each other,
We only follow, follow each other's shadow,
Walking, walking . . . . .
    How many years now,
These shadows walking, these long walking shadows?
On and on, and on and on,
To the wilderness, marching to the Great Wall?
Sounds of bugles, it seems. A big squad of cavalry
Moves on, facing a big circle of morning sun.
The morning sun is each person's red face; horse hooves
Raise golden dust, ten feet, twenty-feet high.
Nothing, nothing at all. I am still on the sidewalk,
Nor do I see the old man of former times; two or three
Soldiers in yellow uniforms standing before the main gate,
(Army headquarters? Once a so-and-so prefecture?)
They stand there upright like tombstones,
Making no sound, no conversation, and thinking of home,

Of home under the sky of the Northeast? Must be. . . . . .
But to think of it now is useless,
Even if they think of the enemy's war horses now
Drinking water by the well of
Their home, or of a group of chickens
Wandering uneasily into sorghum fields, also
Of not knowing where their temporary home be! Thud, thud.
What? Gunshots? Where from?
Local-made guns! Our own! No fear, no fear. . . . . .
But the singing of crickets has already seeped through
The green silk cover, now all faded!
Thinking? Not a bit of use at all!
Think tomorrow. Now do nothing but
Keep quiet, no conversation, but come head-lowered.
Look at the cars flash past the long boulevard.
How "modern"! how comfortable! Martial-looking, eh. . . .
But how can they be compared to the large flags of former times?
A whole face of broad smiles under the red sun!
If you don't believe me, ask the three big red doors
In front, now sadly facing
The autumn sun.
    Ah! under the setting sun
I have an old friend who is living in
A much older city, how is he now?
Perhaps he is walking past a deserted street,
Accompanying a long, slanting, faint shadow?
Tell me your first impressions of Changan.
(By my side there seems to be your shadow)
Friend, don't follow the example of the old man;
Let us talk. . . . . .

Round Jewel Box

Where do I fancy I fathom
A round jewel-box? From the Milky Way?
It contains a few pearls
A drop of transparent watery mercury
Holds the colors and forms of the whole world

A drop of golden lamp
Keeps in it a hall of luxurious feast
A drop of fresh rain
Swells with your last night's sigh
Don't go to a clock & watch store
To listen to your youth being eaten away by silkworms
Don't go to an antique shop
To buy your grandfather's old bric-a-bracs
See, my round jewel-box
Now follows my boat to flow onward
Down, although passengers in the cabin are
Always in the blue sky's embrace
Although your handshakes
Are a bridge—Yes, a bridge, but a bridge
Also built within my jewel-box
And my jewel-box to you
To them, is perhaps
For hanging on the ears, a drop of
A pearl—a precious stone—a star?

Fragment

You stand upon the bridge to look at the landscape.
A landscape viewer upon the tower looks at you.

The moon decorates your window.
You decorate other people's dreams.

The Composition of Distances

Mount a high tower alone to read *The Rise & Decline of the Roman Empire*,
Rome's comet suddenly appears in the newspaper.
Newspaper falls. Map opens. And remember a distant friend's request.
The landscape sent here is already vague with dusk.
(Wake up: sky about to darken. Tedious! Perhaps go see a friend.)
Grey sky. Grey sea. Grey road.
Where now? And I know not how to verify some soil under the lamp.

How tired! Did someone dally with my vessel?
A friend brings here snow and 5 o'clock.
                                        (1935)

White Shell

Empty, spiritual, white shell, you!
No trace of dust within the walls.
Sieved into my hand—
A thousand forms of feelings;
In the palm, loudening surges.
I exclaim: what craftsmanship!
What mind, O Sea!
You are so fine, bead-threading fine.
But I cannot hold myself:
Such an obsession for cleanliness, Ah!

Look at this lake of smoke-rain
Soaking me all over like water
Drenching a bird's feathers.
I am like a small tower.
Winds comb it, catkins comb it,
Swallows comb it like a shuttle.
In the tower are rare books, too,
With pages woven by silver fish,
From the word "love" to "sorrow"
To transcend blind men's flowers.

Crystal-neat, white shell, me!
The sea sends me to the shore.
If I am to fall into men's hands,
Let a primitive man cherish me,
To change for a mountain goat
Still twenty-eight of thirty in need—
Worthy of perhaps a celestial peach.
Only afraid to be picked up by a thoughtful one.
Empty, spiritual, white shell, you
Roll up the tides of my sorrow.

I dream of your jade railings,
Stone-steps drip-drilled by rain-drops,
Well-fence cut open by turning ropes,
Time ground through by patience!
Yellow returns to baby chickens,
Green returns to young sycamores.
Rose to rose plants goes.
But look back by the roadside
Upon the soft thorns of the rose
Still hang your tears of last night.

Untitled (I)

Three days ago a small stream in the mountain
Flashed across a shade of your smile and left.
This morning you met again. You rubbed your eyes:
Before the house, behind the house, what a stretch of spring tide!

A hundred twists, a thousand bends, all untold.
Water has sorrow, sorrow by itself. Water is willing to carry you.
Where is your boat? Where, boat? Go downstairs.
Beyond South Village, in one night, all almond flowers in full bloom.

Untitled (II)

Windows are waiting for an inlay, your leaning on.
So are listless dressing mirrors—how to console?
Silence, a roomful, recalls fixatively, a gold-transforming finger.
A knock upon the door: You come at the right time.

Willow branches beckon people. Spring water teases people.
Kites fly. Fishes frisk. Green mountains, green. White clouds, white.
Upon the lapels, no lack of wrinkles.
What is missing is your right foot—this one beat!

Untitled (III)

I will not forget to carefully clean my soles on your doormat,
So as not to bring travelling dust to ruin your room,
As a token of thanks for your using blotting paper on
Your word-tears to avoid smearing your letter to me.

Doormat has grieving traces; blotting paper has, too.
I understand that sea water can cleanse the world's smoke.
A white handkerchief can at least hold some corals.
But you'd rather see it wave after green flags upon the platform.

Untitled (IV)

Some earth has been mouthed from across the river up to your beams.
Some fountain has been brought from next door into your cup.
Luxury items from abroad now anchored in your chest,
I want to study the history of communications.

Last night, a slice of sigh paid.
This morning, two buds of smiles received.
Paid: a twig of mirror-flower.
Received: a wheel of water-moon.
For you, I have kept a day-to-day account.

Untitled (V)

Walking, I feel grateful
That the buttonhole has its uses,
Because it is empty,
Because it can hold a small flower.

From the pinned flower, I am enlightened
That the world is empty,
Because it has its uses,
Because it allows for your promenade.

City of Spring

City of Spring: Fly a kite upon the garbage dump.
Depict a flower-butterfly, depict an eagle,
In the heart of Madrid's blue sky,
Sky, oceanlike. A pity that one cannot see you,
Oh Kyoto!—

What bad luck! Again another bath of dust!
Cars, you swim in shallow water, but look at this!
What joke are you playing on me?

Sorry! This, this is nothing.
That other is really wild (Indeed, horrid!)
Winds of yellow wool stir up a huge incense-burner.
A thousand years of old old ash
Flies, flies, flies, flies, flies.
Out come horses, out come wolves, out come tigers,
Running, rolling, howling all over the streets,
Pouncing upon your window, spitting upon you,
Pouncing upon your house, downing a corner,
A corner of glazed tiles?—

"Good Lord! Really scared me! Lucky it's not
A bomb—ha! ha! ha!"
"Feels so good: Spring dream dreams into fragrance?
No customer? So what! I will dose off at my pedals.
Lucky that tiles have eyes"
"Bird droppings also have eyes! Ha! ha! ha!"
Ha! ha! ha! What is there to laugh about?
Hysteria, understand? Hysteria!
Sad! Sad!
Sad, indeed! Children mimic old men.
Don't belittle their smallness. Flying a kite upon the garbage dump,
He will also hum: "I remember years back. . . . . . "
Sad! Ancient trees of the whole city
Vainly howl and cry,
Howl and cry, howl and cry.

O Return, O Return
Ancient capital! What can we do to the Ancient Capital!. . . . . .

I am only a kite with a broken string,
Hitting tips of willow branches one is reluctant to have.
You are my home, my tomb,
Wanting to see you fluttering with flowers, fluttering all over,
As my form and shape thin out day by day.
This, it is this alone that is nonsense talk. Sorry, but look!
City of Spring: Fly a kite upon the garbage dump.
The weather yesterday was truly awful.
Whenever spring comes, Mr. Fang always complains, slashing out at the sky even:
Yellow, yellow, a lid upon our heads like a huge tomb.
Mr. Cui: It looks indeed ominous. Just look:
A skyful of dust. Who knows! Maybe after one night of sleep,
We might never see the sky again, and have to wait for centuries
For others to dig us up, but
Today, look, what beautiful weather!
Even the flowering trees on the streets are riding upon unicycles for a spring outing.
After the spring outing, there are peony shows under red-silk lamps.
(At this hour, they are probably enjoying cherry-blossoms?)
In the sky, dove-bells—
Blue sky, white doves, not a trace of airplanes.
Seeing scenery from a plane, I tell you,
Nobody is hard-hearted enough to bomb the glazed tiles below
. . . . . .
City of Peking: Fly a kite upon the garbage dump.

Note by author: Spring, 1934, Peking, two years after the Japanese amassed their troops against China. As for Madrid, I vaguely remember that Kuriyagawa Hakuson once said: Peking is like Madrid. As for Kyoto, it is totally free association, because it is literally next door to Peking. As a matter of fact, the sky of Kyoto is not at all blue; this, I found out later.

The Migrating Birds Problem

How many courtyards to how many pieces of blue sky?
I let you people divide them. I have to go.
Let white doves with bells fly three rounds above our heads,
But camel bells are already far away. Listen!
Swing a top to stay you, fly a kite to pull you,
Or let paper-eagles, paper-swallows, paper-cocks, three or four,
Fly up to the sky—up to meet the southward geese?
And are we, do you think, toys of these children?
But go to a library to borrow a copy of *The Migrating Birds Problem*
Now, did you or did you not approve
The city's ordinance to ban airplanes from the city sky?
My thoughts are like the webbing strings small spiders ride upon,
Tying my feet to fly me, to float me. I have to go.
Forget it now until return.
How many courtyards to how many pieces of blue sky?
How can I be like a desperate radio,
Doing nothing but stretching two arms above the roof,
Failing to catch the distant waves we want.

He Qifang (1912–1977)

Autumn

Shaking down dewdrops dabbling all morning,
Sounds of timber-cutting float out from dark valleys.
Laying down sickles sated with fragrances of grains
And plump fruits, melons from wattles carried in back-baskets,
Autumn rests in a farmer's home.

Casting round nets into the cold mists on the river,
Pulling in blue-bream-shaped black tallow shadows
With reed-awnings white-frosted
Autumn returns, rowing light oars
And plays upon the fishing boat.

The meadow becomes more silent with crickets singing.
The stream, more limpid with rocks emerging from drying water
Where have the flutes upon ox-backs gone?
Where, the flute-holes brimming with summer night's heat scent?
Autumn dreams in the eyes of a shepherdess.
                                        1932

Don't Wash the Red*

Lonely beating of the wash-stone fills the cold pond.
Clear ancient waves tremble with the beating.

---

* Name of a tone-pattern used by Ci (*tz'u*) poets of the Song Dynasty.

My weary arm hangs down.
What can it pick up from the golden-green?

Footfalls of spring, shadows of merriment
Fade stealthily with the fading of silk wear.
Frequently washed by sunshine, rains and winds,
Wouldn't crimson dreams also fade?

I beat the wash-stone: cold autumn light approaches.
Its feet, soaked in ice-cold water,
Tread the white frost upon the plank-bridge,
Making my shadow shiver in the reflection.

The Cypress Grove

Sunlight upon the large leaves of castor-oil plants,
Seven-mile bees in the nest of the Tutelar Temple,
I, a runner with shadows,
Return from rounding a huge circle
To find time standing still.

But on green green grass
Where now, the short arms that once chased after singing crickets
Where, the happy shouts of playmates
That reached the blue sky beyond treetops?
This enormous childhood kingdom
Dwindles pitifully
Under my feet laden with exotic dust.

To a desert traveller, a cup of water is gold.
To a boatman, high waves upon oars are to be grieved.
I thought before that I had a paradise
Snugly stored away in the dark cove of my memory.
Now I feel the loneliness of adults
And fall in love with the mist on roads in dreams.

Night Scene (1)

City noises subside
Like tides receding from the beach.
Under each grey roof
Lie some sleeping souls.

The last old horse-carriage is gone.

Outside the palace door some laborers
Are sleeping upon large stone-slabs.
Waking up at midnight, they kick their companions,
Saying that they heard some weeping
Far and near, near and far,
From the tightly locked deserted palace,
From the turret all taken over by crows.
Stranger are the anwers:
That one evening
They saw tears coming out of eyes of stone lions . . . . . .

Fading into the distance with soft sighs,
Night winds shake the dying grass upon the citadel.

Night Scene (II)

In the blue mist, a thin moon at its last quarter.
(If you are not a stranger in the city,
You might mistake one person for another).

Horse-hooves' splitting sound in death-threatening silence.
Before the corroded red door,
Under a half circle of yellow lamp,
A tremulous hand opens the car door,
And lets down a black shadow
Who feels his way to the brass door-knockers.
Knock, knock, two feeble attempts.
(He must be a wanderer, you say.
Having thrown away emptily half of his life,

He now returns to this ravaged courtyard,
Or is he, drooping old, homeless, returning
From faraway to seek refuge with his last kin?)
Two knocks upon the brass door-knockers
Press for an answer to this weird silence inside,
(Or for an answer to his indeterminate fate?)
The corroded red door opens,
Lets in the shadow and shuts
(And shuts you out in the world.)
Horse-hooves' splitting sound fades into the distance.

(Thus, toward evening,
Birds begin to take wings
For fear that in the deep dark night
They might find the wrong nests in the forest.)

Burial

The white candle burning in silence
Is the sigh forced out from our bosom.
This is the age of burials.

I hear bad-tempered Lord Byron,
With the tingling of ice, say: "Money,
Money is tingling cold, but it can buy pleasures."

I see Nerval pull along on the street a lobster,
Who knows marine secrets, with a blue ribbon
And, with the sash of an apron,
Hang himself outside the door of a penny-a-night hotel.
At last, the pastoral poet inside the hotel
Cuts the blue veins upon his neck with a knife.

I sing no more of love
The way summer cicadas sing of the sun.

Adjectives, metaphors and manmade paper flowers
Can only glimmer once in the furnace.
The silkworms that silently eat pages of your books
Are not sluggard in making their cocoons.
This is winter.

In the long long funeral procession
I bury myself
Like the myth-sowing huge serpent whose teeth
Grew into a host of armored fighters
That attacked each other
Until only one remained, the strongest.

1936

Clouds

"I love clouds . . . . . . the clouds which pass by . . . . . ."
I thought of myself as that man in Baudelaire's prose poem
Who raised his neck melancholily
Looking into the distant sky.

I walked into the rural area.
Peasants lost their land because they were honest,
Their home reduced to a bundle of farming tools.
In the daytime, they went to the fields to find odd jobs.
At night, they slept on dry hard stone bridges.

I walked into the city by the sea.
Upon the tar streets of winter
Rows and rows of apartments stand
Like modern prostitutes upon the sidewalks
Waiting for pleasures of summer
And pot-bellied lust and shamelessness.

From now on, I will make loud comments:

I'd rather have a thatched roof;
I don't love clouds, nor moon,
Nor stars.

                        1937 Spring

Cao Baohua (1906–1978)

From *Fugitive Stanzas*

II.2

A little monk on a bicycle
Passes the ancient Forbidden City.
He goes round and round the Tutelar Altar,
This, you say, is worthy of surprise.

No wonder the bald-headed old man
Sitting on a bench in the park
Looking at young lovers, hand-in-hand, pass by,
Would stroke his beard, sighing, "O long time ago . . . . . ."

Long time ago someone under the moon
Dreamt of the palace in the heavens
And saw afterwards before the Mirror of Sins
Even shadows would turn into dust.

Into dust! What is the difference?
Hurry up! Go now to the flyover.
Under the sun, shadows tread on shadows,
Vying to see women turned into men.

II.3

Waking up from a cold dream at dawn,
I hear in the distance the sawing of wood,
Busily building a coffin, it seems,
Waiting for me, this strange man
Who spends a whole life drinking from his brain.

Dare think no more. Every time when the sunset
Sprinkles red blood upon the wild grass,
When I walk past the old old cemetery gate,
Some hand would stretch out to pull me—
A sudden heartbeat, a trembling in the body.

I would rather be a creature of no knowledge,
(Be anything at all but man)
Trying in deep mountains of time immemorial,
To watch day in day out a shadow
Walk past and slowly return.

Boast not the five carts of books in your mind,
That you can see through the star's secrets.
In no time would the footfalls from downstairs
Hand you a soul-extortion bill—
Quick! Pull your head back into your dream.

II.6

A Daoist monk blows his magic conch skyward
Calling into deep mountains a host of lions
Suddenly turned into stones; they stare hard into the sand—
Babylon now sunk into oblivion for five thousand years,
Leaving dead corpses on the ground.

Feeling his side, he finds the sun and moon
Inside the gourd gone: how now to guide fingers
To knock on doors distantly locked in dreams?
The skyward cap falls from his head.
On the level ground surges a deluge.

Heavy bags, dragging hooves toward the western sky,
The black donkey sighs on its way
Over a thousand, ten thousand mountains.
A million acres of sand weighs on the eyelids —-
As a lone star glitters beyond the sky . . .

II.10

One stone breaks up the heaven-earth in the water.
Over our heads suddenly float here several white doves.
A piece of feather, two bridges of rainbow.
Beyond a million miles someone is lost in thought:
A dream? A morning star falling off the sky?

We pick up our shadows and walk into double doors.
Ten thousand thunders stop abruptly at our feet.
A pinch of yellow earth*, two lines of tears.
Upon the ancient cliff flashes a bright red name.
A declining soul kneels down to weep.

---

* With associations of the underworld.

Zhang Kejia (1910-)

Refugees

The sun has fallen into the birds' nests.
The afterglow has not yet dissolved the wings of returning crows.
Strange roads and the anchorless dusk
Have led these people to this ancient town.
Heavy shadows planted both sides of the main street,
Clusters by clusters, like haystacks on autumn fields,
Silent, solitary, arch out a cosmic sorrow.
Their tattered clothes laden with journey's dust
Speak their origins;
Their shadow-infested faces
Tell their conditions.
Spiralling cooking smoke evokes a flight of longing eyes
And pulls out from their hearts an unthinkable thought:
"At this moment, the afterglow is hesitating among old tree tops,
Spreading from smokeless roofs to infinity
As ghostly sorrow swallows up their pitiful native town."
Strong fatigue, together with body and thought, is pushed into a mist.
But stronger hunger immediately brings them back to this alien town,
Like a devil falling among these people from a dream,
A grey shadow's hand is flashing a rifle,
Whose small voice explodes into a boom in their ears:
"The times are bad. We dare not let any living person stay in town!"
"Alas, wherever people go, disasters are with them!"
A series of sighs: the dusk is even darker.
Step by step, these people walk past the main street
And take leave of this alien town.
The cries of small children derange the hearts of adults.

The banging of iron-gates cut off the last person's footfall,
When the afterglow climbs over the stonewalls of the ancient town.

1932

Life

This is no fooling around fun; this is life.
A million arrows lie in ambush around you,
Waiting for your one careless moment from a thousand vigilant ones.
Disasters are constellations in the sky
Whose light pulls along your fate.
Hope is a mere sunray through the crevice of black clouds,
Is the last illumination in a patient's eyes.
Who is willing to push oneself to an impasse?
Those happy things, one, and then another,
(Real? Unreal? Who can tell?)
Are a broken rainbow dyed on the western sky,
Only this is real, for life's very struggles
Have left in your heart ponderous pains.
It would teach you to know life upon needles,
And heighten your spirit with a mere sound
(Even if it were spring winds over spring flowers)
Like a warrior who thinks of war in the neighing of horses.
Then you would never say to yourself again:
"Life is but a rootless dream."
Nor would you complain that you were greatly wronged
And spit out all kinds of curses at a mere mosquito's bite.
In life's scenario, since you are a role assigned,
Go for it, regardless of risks; play it to your heart's content,
And make people rise and fall with your moods.
Forget even that you are playing,
Since you have the guts to come into this world,
Whatever feats you have, worry not; they will be used.
The grating and grinding of now is your opponent
Against whom you should exert full strength to fight,
Tired out though with sweat dotting all the pores,
Against whom you must bite tight your teeth, never to slacken.

In the meantime, you should be in fear of overcoming it,
Of the void left behind by the loss of an opponent.
In this way, you could live somewhat stubbornly
With much bitterness, yes, but bitterness with your unique flavor.

1933

Old Horse

Get the cart fully packed, they say,
Since this thing says not a word!
The weight on its back cuts into its flesh
And down hangs its ponderous head.

This moment knows not what fate the next portends.
Its tears, if any, all inward go.
A whip flashes across its eyes;
It raises its head to look forward.

1932

Laborers Taking a Noon Break

Laying down work,
They lay down everything,
They want to sleep—
Sleep:
Spread the earth as bed.
Pull the sun as cover,
Head pillowing upon scattering shades,
The hand of one lying on the bosom of another.
A body hair
Holds a dangling bead of sweat
Inside which is lighted up unrestricted comfort.
Under the sun, upon the iron-colored skin
Now bloom a field of white flowers.
Rough snoring is
Keeping measure with breathing.
Iron wings in deep sleep have now covered their heart,

Blocking even a light dream to come closer.
When they have slept silently
Over this tiring noon hour,
They will jump up, shake themselves,
And swell with a body of new strength.

1933

A Warrior's Heart

The night in the river temple declines with the oil lamp.
The dream of a warrior is flowering in brilliant colors,
Pillowing on a book on the art of war and a sword.
The light flowers into a head of white hair.

Suddenly he opens his eyes wide, war-drums urging.
(Inside the hall, one note chases another on the wood-chime.)
He walks out; stars very much resemble those of old.
Upon the iron-mails resound cold winds of the Northern Pass.

Before him clearly are millions of horses galloping.
He waves his sword and cries a loud loud cry.
Since then the warrior has never returned.
Before the door, river tides pound night after night.

1934

Xin Di (1912–)

Sail

The sail is set.
Verging toward where the sun sinks.
Bright-clean against the old
Windblown sail smacking the dark water
Like black butterfly, white butterfly.

Bright moon shines vertically on our head
Green snake
Playing the silver-pearls.
Whispers upon the wind
Blown over by the wind
The sailors ask about rains, about stars.

From day till night,
From night till day,
We cannot sail out of this circle.
Behind, a circle.
In front, a circle.
An eternal
Rimless circle.

Take the mist off life
For the mist of smoke-water.

(1934)

Afternoon in Autumn

Sunlight is like rolls and rolls of torn silk.
Upon the pane is reflected the cold, white distant river.
Those slender slender
Hands of insects feet of insects
How much coldness do they pick up?
The light of years gradually goes.

(1936)

Remembering

How many gorgeous sunsets
Can one have in one's life?
The dovecalls of distant sky
Bring here words of remembrance.
Cowering reedcatkins all white-headed,
One year is going to end.
Roads under the City Wall are solitary.
Deep red, all the trees,
Falling, scattering: fit only for self-ruminating.
Travellers disappear into the distance in the autumn wind.

July, 1934

Outside the Door

    The silk is stilled.
    The jade steps are dust-laden.
    The empty room is cold, lonely.
    Fallen leaves cling to the closed door.

The night is here,
Stepping with a cat's steps.
Don't let the dust and the spider's web upon the door web you
Let the key turn itself in the long-locked lock,
A guest? or the host?
Coming in this year's end, winter's end,
From afar

With, moreover, a remembering heart.
I am happy.
My eyes can still see
Shadows and shapes of darkness,
Still holding one or two
White flowers, yellow flowers.
I still remember the "plop-plop" in the fireplace,
Because of the chestnuts we threw in,
Or was it new sawn firewood.
So distant, years and months.
Between the fingers playing with flowered hairpins,
How many pale piano notes
Had flowed over?
But outside the door is nothing but a locked road,
Rains and snows three days long.
I no longer hear you say, "O how haggard!"
I only want to lightly
Write on the dust-covered mirror an "I".
I only want the purple light cup
To touch once more my lips of love.
But I fear
Fear that everything is going to break into powder instantly.
Here, there is no more waiting,
Or not waiting.
Tonight, like last night, the same dead still.
The red and silver candlelight
Will no longer lengthen or turn green for me.
I cannot hear the words of the eyes,
Twenty years twenty years
I have never found the familiar jade-pendants.
Upon the cat's steps,
Night comes.
One, two
White flowers, yellow flowers.
It seems that I am lost with everything
In this winter's end, year's end,
Coming from afar
With, moreover, a remembering heart.

Old Musician

Already stilled, the strings.
Listen: this very one is ringing.

In a dead water pond,
A feather upon the green stains
Has a message from beyond the sky.
But after all the suffering as a drifter,
Where is the worth of living?

That drip-drip drip-drip,
I don't think is my tears.

1937–38

Dujuan Flower and Bird*

April by April, Browning's homesick April,
On a misty island I see this flower strong and bright,
(Oh, it has also travelled far from old China)
Evokes within my heart
The wail of this bird from my native country my native town.
You must know, grief is the fate we share,
But I am a dumb one by the road,
All the more stubborn and unbending.
Today alone I run aimlessly through the empty mountains.
Restless, my heart churns out old sentiments that lead me to find
The flowing stream in the grass.
I do not expect to hear you again ahead of me against the wind,
Waking my past dreams within layers of dreams.

---

* The title "Dujuan Flower and Bird" literally means "Azalea and Cuckoo", but both the flower and the bird share the same name "Dujuan" in Chinese. In Chinese legends, the Dujuan bird is the soul of an ancient emperor whose sad sound of crying is capable of invoking home-sick feelings from travellers. The Dujuan flower is believed to have attained its bright red color from the spilt blood of a young girl who died of an ill-fated love.

Thank you for warmly telling me that you have also come south,
But you and I are the same and not the same,
You always pass and do not stay,
In bright moonlight you will still fly through dense waters, crowded hills;
And I, this overseas traveller, modern man from China,
Seeing that for you the East and the West are but the same world.
Could only close my palms in generous praise.

(Translated by Leung Pingkwan)

A Poet in Paris

Idling girl at the sidewalk cafe
Etoile, her daily home.
Clouds in the sky sink into a cup of black coffee,
Glittering in the deep mire of her soul.
Wide open window
Quietly gives upon
The antique variegated Seine.
The air of each autumn is transparent like water.
Silk clothes in their lightness unknowingly touch upon
A coldness, and, impartially, upon the visitor from afar.
This metropole de fleurs is a beautiful tree one never gets tired of
But now Europa declines,
Overgrown with bacteria
And the voices from the *France-Soir* are too tense.
Who can be like an ostrich
Burying his head inside the snake-skin dream of the Persian Dance,
To hide the turmoil of this world?
Before coming here one kept demanding to come.
Now we are here, what is special about it?
A thousand miles, a million miles,
My heart simply cannot be changed by this exotic charm
And forget about the Mountain Pass moon of my bleak nation.
Whatever you can do, give me a wall, a clearing,
I would sit down cross-legged,
Make myself a new man out of earth,

Or, as with nirvana, a Buddha,
To work faithfully, conscientiously,
Like a convict waiting to die.
But
I have come into this world positively
To welcome this new century.

Good-by, Blue Horse Inn

Time to go
The host of Blue Horse Inn said to me.

—Let me see you off.
Let me raise up a lamp.
See: upon the door, your shadow, my shadow.
See: one night, all frost upon the wooden bridge

Let fall
This night wind   This road under star light.
The horse raises its head to chew the branches.
This is autumn of white dews.
He does not know these are not transparent grapes.
The cock crows,
But sunlight is not here.
Madrid's blue sky is already under the wings of war,
Seven colors changed into three
Black   Red   Purple
The end is but a world of winds and fires.
Listen: the blacksmith next door is pulling his bellows again.
The rise and fall of his arm's sinews
Speak well of his creative strength.
Is it the wide night or the miracle before you
That has kept you up all the night and not to sleep?
Come or go, you want to be with Don Quixote,
But except for windmills   except for giants
The jungles are overgrown with creepers   flutes of devils
How long have I been this way,

A walking staff and my lone shadow?

—Young man, though not a festival,
You should have a share of joy.
You are not in want of new clothes, new hats.
Why do you always envy other children?
Walk on with some pride.
Goodby   safely
Goodby   young guest
Goodby means   "God be with you"

1937

One Day at Bear Mountain

Outside traces of eight million people,
Unexpectedly I found this secluded place.
Flowing water washes my emotions pure and clear,
Green forests paint my life with joy and freshness.
At the Seven-Bend Lake, pleasant birdsongs
Allow me to have three springs in one day.

Wild begonia flowers fall: no one notices.
Time stays upon pine needles.
White clouds unfurl as they please.
If only I could have this leisure of a stopover visitor,
But calls of distressed times have split my heart.
Now I cannot. Now I cannot.

1948
Outside New York City.

Wu Xinghua (1921–1966)

The Woman who plays the pipa lute

He would not notice this composition—to him
The past is like a moth-eaten dustladen curtain
Rolled up, put aside. Only when an instant
Is isolated in Time's torrent can he taste deeply
The liquor of life's cup. Meanwhile, I try hard
To make the present bear the entire weight of the past,
To make the past alive in the present—happiness, hope,
Long years' wait, contemplation beyond this world
All seem to rush toward my fingers, the strings shrilly
Cry out: We cannot bear . . . . . .

Mentor from the Capital and other players often praised my
Mastery: "Even in dreams you would not make mistakes!"
Yes! Mastery: Fingers and plectrum all blend
Into one, threatening, imploring, seducing
To release all the hidden sounds and voices;
This needs skill and thousands of sleepless nights,
But only today I seem to fully sense the very
Meaning of this composition. The moon amidst the river
Opens up my heart: Crystal clear, inside and outside.

March. Rains freshly stopped. Upon the King Wei Dam
Handsome horses galloped, avoiding slippery spring soil.
He held my hand, smiling: "We will meet again."
Clamorous pipes continued as some guests
Gathered around a willow tree pacifying a girl—
The flower on her hair pinned way off—"Afterall
The amber plate isn't worth much. Don't

Grieve over its breaking." We were then young,
Our lives stretching afar beyond our ken.
"Mistakes can be patched. Lost chances
Will beckon again." I did not answer,
And, with eyes' corners wetting, saw him leave.

The scars months and years carved upon his forehead
Were like the debits upon the board in the wineshop
Line after line: "When can you clear these debits?"
"I will return and erase all these, and will,
With a clean slate, begin again." He said.
Now he stared into the distance, let the music enter
Mistily into his breast, his limbs, ready to grasp
That which nobody can grasp, bidding it to stay . . . . . .
Would he explain in his heart these sounds
And, in the infinitely complex and dazzling crossways,
Seek out that which is concealed but real?
Music, that winged immortal, please lend me
Sincere colors, let the sufferings of half of my life
Like the single leaf upon the highest branch
Bathe in the sun, unfold timidly, reach beyond
The invisible walls around and make him remember . . . . . .

O O my selfsame hands and fingers, my changed mood,
Striving to disclose from beneath the smooth composition
My very self. Cold ice, hard cold ice,
And beneath, in the darkness, slowly runs a live river.
Can he tell from it this fine fine difference? When
My desperate cry is filled with this wide wide space,
Listening, did he still hear only that familiar tune.
He had been tired of hearing: "Echo of masters of the Capital"?

The boat is about to leave. The beginning of their voyage
Happens to be the end of mine. Within this composition,
I have buried everything. Brief, evanescent.
This is music's but also my destiny.
Wine and hot tears drench his sleeves.
But who knows for what he is sorrowful?

Perhaps music has liberated him from
His own circle. Among the things he sees
There is also my little share. If this instant
Can find an eternal memory in his poetry,
I would be content to retreat into whistling
Bamboos in the underworld, like a shooting star, leaving
No name, but an instant flash breaking darkness . . . . . .

To Eva

Eva, while living, let us think of the flowers
About to wither tomorrow. All the wasted labor today
Would be sorrowful tears one finds, looking back, when
New fragrances float by the hair of beautiful girls?
Parted by a moonlit window, I look down. Breezes
Come and go in the middle of the street. And you stand
Silently in the garden, a statue, symbol of lasting beauty
Out of this world, unsoiled indeed by a pinch of dust —
And I, a dreaming poet, see in your brightness
A fleeting love, and how desire can transcend
The limits of knowledge on a distant journey, like a meteorite,
To visit "worlds" unheard, unseen by man.

I don't know how many years ago, when quiet night clouds
Encroached upon the pale ring of the moon and thin mist
Pet the plains, Xi Shi* was listening to the winds
In the tree-filled corridor. What was she thinking? Who would know?
For her snow-colored complexion alone, a king would even
Topple his own rising, still unfolding state!
Even when in melancholy she leaned on the jade bed,
He should notice in her eyes those staghorn does
Would come to trample his palace. Unsurpassed beauty

---

* After King Yue was defeated by King Wu (between 700–476 B.C.), Fan Li, prime minister of Yue, offered a beautiful girl Xi Shi as a temptress, a sort of femme fatale, to King Wu and subsequently toppled him. Legend has it that, after King Wu's fall, Fan Li retired from the turmoil of politics and went a-boating with Xi Shi.

Immersed in thoughts. The Universe was still too limited;
Between her lips hung the fates of the States of Wu and Yue.
She was oblivious to success and failure. Man would be
Content just to receive her responses, be they cold, indifferent.
Her soul sought for things that were more distant.
More mysterious
    —or nonexistent at all.
People, curious, often ask: After Gusu fell,
Xi Shi and Fan Li, where did they drift to?
Only undisturbed beauty is complete.
A mere word would lessen her manifold delicate charm.
Since she was not born from this ponderous Earth,
Why should she be concerned about change in status?
From the brow-knitted Queen to the wife of a drifting
Boatman, she kept her silence, accepted
Different embraces with the same worried mood.
Day in day out she breathed the unfamiliar air of this world.
Never once did she not feel that she was a mere passer-by.

O pitiable space! What has taken us by surprise
Is nothing but a dot of dust. She might have seen
Or intuitively felt such a thing that by comparison
Everything else is like flowing water, and her a rock,
A steadfast rock in the water for millions of years,
Listening to new waves overcoming old waves before and behind,
While she kept herself in an everlasting divine silence.

But Eva, in your life, you do not have worries
For the future, so long as time still places
Her jade-like feet on the mountains of human world.
Your silence is the symbol of countless girls of no name
In history, although you are born in the present.
Day in day out the soul is always like court ladies kept
In the Everlasting Lane dreaming the fragrant spring beyond this
  world.

A Sketch

The grade school at lane's end closes
At 5 p.m. Silence, with broad strides, returns,
Except a few sobs from small children
Lingering there.

Cooking smoke all still in midair.
Tree leaves, like a troop of grey mice,
Climb the steps of air, up, up and up,
And then, headfirst, fall down.

Lighted, the small store is energized again—
A woman in a white apron,
Broom hitting the ground,
Scolds a dog lost in meditation.

The moon, a barely bright button
In night's light blue bra,
Has, however, an unusually enchanting light,
Rising as it does to decorate the flag in the school yard.

Mu Dan (1918–1977)

The Lyric in the Air Raid Shelter

Laughing, he said to me: Here is cool!
I wiped off the sweat, brushed the dirt from climbing the hill.
All the time I saw his slim body
Trembling, in a draft of wind underground.
He laughed and said: You should not miss this chance, have fun!
This is the Shen Daily from Shanghai. All this colorful news!
Let's sit over there, there's a ray of dim light.
I thought of the people running madly in the streets,
Those cruel people, threatened by death,
Like swarms of insects, squeezed into our shelter.

Who knows what seeds farmers planted in this earth?
I was sleeping in the tall buildings, one said, I was taking a bath.
Do you expect the stock market to go up? You live at . . . . . .?
Oh, Oh, I'll drop by some other time; I'm terribly busy lately.
Silence. They seemed to have felt the lack of oxygen,
Though the underground was safe. Each one was watching the other:
Oh, black faces, black bodies, black hands!
Then I heard the gust in the sun
Wrapping around everyone whispering gentle calls,
From his roof, from his books, from his blood.

    The alchemist lowered his heavy
    Eyelids, fell unconsciously into dreams.
    Countless spirits were out from hell,
    Hid quietly, the fire burning, the skin yet to husk,
    Listened to the tunes from the country of Ultimate Pleasure.

Oh, look, in the great forest of ancient times,
The vampire which had gradually frozen!

I stood up. Here the air is too suffocating.
I said: It's finished, let's get out!
But he held me by the arm: Look, isn't this your good friend?
She got married in a Shanghai Hotel? Here's the announcement!

I had forgotten to pick a white lilac to put between the pages.
I had forgotten to wave a walking-stick in the park,
Drifting under the neon lights, listening to "Love Parade,"
I had forgotten to use pale violet ink to write, to add a slice of lemon
   to my tea.
When you lowered your head, and raised it again,
You saw so many people in front of your eyes, you saw so many on the
   plain,
You saw the countless people, whom you didn't see again,
Then you felt yourself stained in black, like all the others.

That vampire was turning in pain,
He got up quietly to light the crucible,
In the pitch dark night of the ancient forest,
"Destroy! Destroy!" a voice cried,
"You futile old crucible!
Die in dream! Fall into pain!
How strong is your voice of Ultimate Pleasure!"

Who has won? He asked, and has several enemy planes shot down?
I laughed and said: I have.
When people returned home, dusting off the grass and mud,
From the great net woven above their heads,
I was alone going up the stairs of the shelled building,
And discovered that I was lying dead in there,
Stiffened, with a face of joy, tears and sighs.

April, 1939
(Translated by Leung Pingkwan)

"I"

Cut off from the womb, all warmth lost,
I am a torn part yearning for rescue,
Always a single self locked in wilderness.

From still dreams I left the group,
And pained in time's flow, clutching at nothing.
Continuous memories cannot bring back my self.

The metamorphosed image is deeper desperation,
Always a single self locked in wilderness,
Hating mother for parcelling out a separate dream.

1940

Protest

I

Winter's cold gathers here, friend,
To a child, a melancholy season,
As he still carries the smile of spring.
When rebels pass through fallen leaves,

Quivering, belittled, proud of their own blood,
Why has the world become tattered in oblivion?
Gone, gone, each other's greetings,
And the atmosphere of deep faiths.

Walking upon homeless land,
Wading through experience, lost souls
Find no rest in a certain slant of warmth.
In vain, pains of nostalgia.

Some, with heart's windows closed,
Bracing the wind, walk a failed road,
Though faithful they are to all situations.
Spring's flowers fall behind time.

Because our background is people in millions,
Tragic, passionate, or full of folly,
They fight abreast with fear.
Selfish, those cities to be protected.

We see countless rats, people—
Evading, scheming, walking out,
Dominating the valiant, or, by contributions,
Earning the high honor of "society's pillars".

We can see, this very stance
Is stronger than any ideal. It, alone, is
Indestructible in war. Obedience. Applause. Suffering.
The only responsibility of a weeping conscience—

Silent. Before this background,
Cold winds blow into today and tomorrow.
Cold winds shatter our permanent
Homes, as well as our transitory inns.

II

What do we do? What do we do?
Life continuously tempts us
To desire, in miseries, the snare of happiness,
Alas, for once only; it never comes again:

And will to revenge finally allows
Our own happiness to stamp, legally, upon
The contempt, insult and hostility of others,
Though collapsed in each other's injuries.

Or half-dead? Invading desires of each day,
Separate it, force it to feed on rottenness.
If there is a statue in your heart,
Carve it, carve it with your leftover strength.

Newspapers will startle it every day
And threaten it to go with the flow,
Or perhaps it can bear no longer
And fall to the grimaces of the Age.

But being uncertain if it will become tomorrow's god,
We pain whole days, whole nights.
Piecemeal knowledge makes us distrust
Love in blood, and, for its lack,

We try to mend, ending up in self-exile,
Doing nothing, having faith in nothing.
Clouded days, in expectation of knowledge,
We think of those strengthening youthful days.

This is death. Contradiction in history oppresses us,
Balances and poisons each of our impulses.
The blind would just give vent to their thoughts,
But wisdom enfeebles us, making us impotent.

What do we do? What do we do?
O who should be responsible for these crimes?
Within a common man are hidden
Countless murders, countless births.

       October, 1941

Spring

Green flames flickering upon the grass,
He thirsts to embrace you, flower.
Rebelling earth, flower stretches out,
As warm winds bring trouble or merriness.
If you wake up, open the window
To see how beautiful this full garden of desires.

Under the blue sky, obsessed by an eternal enigma is
Our tightly-closed body of 20-year-old,
Just like birdsongs earth-cast.
You are kindled, curled, but find no home.
O light, shade, sound, color, all now naked,
And in pain, waiting to enter into new combinations.

1942

Cracks

I

Every morning, this quiet street
Is unaware of sufferings to arrive,
Cries of children, the defenseless, silent
Steps of every laborer,
And skyreaching buildings cast huge shadows,
Mixing dirtiness into the primal sunlight.

Skirts, nobler than any labor,
Still quietly possess last night's world.
Crowds, squeezed to the margin by the center,
Step accurately into rooms of eight hours.
These, we see, are a scheme
To mature us together with the daily sunshine.

II

Twisted and twisted, this redhot band
Is finally stamped all over his body.
Those with wings fly. Those with sunlight
Grow. He pursues and falls into darkness.
Four walls are tradition. The dynamic
Daytime upholds all achieved customs.

New hopes are repressed, twisted.

No safety until all is crushed.
Young ones learn to be clever. The aging
Continue their folly.
Who spares the future? Nobody
Would pain themselves.
What changes tomorrow is already changed by today.

June, 1944

Eight Poems

1.

Your eyes saw this fire.
You did not see me, although I kindled it for you.
Ai! What is burning is but the mature age,
Yours, mine. We are separated like mountains.

Of the metamorphoses in Nature's process,
I fell in love with a transitory you.
I may weep, turn to ashes and be reborn,
Dear lady, this is only God toying with himself.

2.

Water flowed between mountain rocks, sedimenting you and me.
And we grew up in the womb of death.
Within countless possibilities, a life of protean change
Will never complete itself.

I talked with you, trusted you, loved you.
Now I hear the Lord laugh secretly.
Continuously, he adds other you's and me's,
Making our life doubly rich and dangerous.

3.

The little beast in your age
Breathed like spring grass.

It brought out your color, fragrance and fullness.
It made you go crazy in warm darkness.

I passed over the marbled hall of reason,
And treasured its buried life therein.
Your hand my hand touched a field of grass.
In it, its obstinacy, my surprised delight.

4.

Quietly, we embraced ourselves within
A world illuminated only by language.
Darkness still-born was horrid.
The possible, the impossible obsessed us.

What suffocated us was
The sweet language that died before it was born.
Its ghost was a lid to force us to drift
Into the freedom, into the beauty of disorderly love.

5.

Westering sun: a breeze flutters the fields.
How ancient were these reasons accumulated here?
What moved the scenery moved my heart
To flow toward you, quiet sleep, from the oldest source.

That which shaped the trees and erected the rocks
Will eternalize my desire of this moment.
All the beauty thus revealed in the process
Will teach me the way to love you, the way to change.

6.

Sameness and sameness dissolve into ennui.
Between differences is congealed strangeness.
Upon so dangerously narrow a road
I have manufactured myself to travel.

He exists, to listen to my commands.
He is protective, but leaves me inside solitude.
His pain is his constant search for
Your order which, when achieved, he must discard.

7.

Storms. Distant roads. Lonely nights.
Loss. Remembrance. Continuous time.
Against the fear that no science can dispel
Let me have restfulness in your breast.

Oh, upon your unindependent heart,
The seen-then-unseen form of beauty,
There, I saw your solitary love
Spear up, growing parallel with mine.

8.

There is no nearer contact.
All the coincidences have taken shape between us.
Only the sun through the abundant leaves
Divides itself equally on two leaves of the same heart.

When the season comes, each will fall its way,
But the giant tree that has given us life will remain forever green.
And his unkind laugh at us (as well as weeping)
Will be transformed into peacefulness in the old roots all in one.

Flag

We are all underneath. You flutter in high sky.
Wind is your body. You walk with the sun,
Always trying to fly beyond, always pulled back by the earth.

Words written on the sky, recognized by everyone,
Simple, clear, and invisibly large,
Souls of heroes alive today.

Your tiny body is the dynamic of wars.
After the war, you are the only whole.
We become ashes; glory is retained by you.

Everybody's mind, but cleverer than everybody,
You come with mornings, and suffer with nights.
You speak fluently the happiness of freedom.

Tempests from four directions, you are the first to feel.
The direction of everybody; because of you victory is set.
We all love you, and to the people you belong.

May, 1945

Du Yunxie (1918–   )

Encampment

Tonight I suddenly discover
In a tree a different beauty:
It opens up for me
A sky of pure, blue silk.

Between confused leaves
Stars strive to grow.
Bare, bald twigs are holding
The roundest gold moon.

A leaf wafts and falls down
Like a face from afar.
It hits the ground with a "zap".
I hear then whispers of the wind.

Winds come from distant villages
With the shyness of a rustic.
Dogs, cold, sneeze. Men, all vengeance.
Cows lean on each other, trembling.

Two humorous blackbirds
Mimic humans to snore,
Laugh aloud suddenly,
And fly into the misty mountains.

So many enthusiastic insects
Take me as their best listener

And play to me their new tunes.
So pessimistic are they I am hurt.

The jeep is beside my pillow,
My rifle all intact, also my clothes.
They are in numb silence.
I rather like this honesty.

Night is deep. My heart is deeper.
In the depth it is normally colder
With more pressure. My heart, smitten,
Wants to be a rooster and cry out loud.

Moon

Age has not lessened
Your feminine charm.
Faithful, pure love is,
(A whole earth of dreamy eyes)
Tonight, same as old times.

Scientists have invented lies
About you: a small star,
Cold, no human color,
And you have charmed millions
Only with the aid of the sun.

In the day you always hide away,
At night you come out all clean,
Followed by bright-eyed stars,
Wandering around till daybreak.
You sneeze before returning home.

But lies have not lessened
Our hungry love for you:
Electric light is merely electric light.
You stir up a flood of feelings
With all kinds of time and scenery.

Two young lovers, petal-like,
Waft to the lawn by the river, sing
An old Hollywood song, and recite
An occasional verse. The pale river
Glimmers, flowing away with garbage.

Alien soldiers, like dead leaves,
Are caught by the bridge-railing on one side.
They recite Li Bai's lines, chewing
"*Lowering head to think of home*"
As if home were a piece of gum.

Tattered coolies, like tattered clothes,
Discarded by the road, make a fire,
Half-dead, remain silent. Leftover glimmers
Upon branches leap upon the faces to
Seek, in vain, poetic lines.

Like a boat carrying refugees, I drift
Upon the asphalt road.
No home behind me.
Are there beaches ahead?
Look at the sky. Tell feelings from dogs' barking.

Tonight, like other nights,
We are crammed on earth.
You, composed like a woman, scan
The strange feelings down below, with the
Shyness of a grand-daughter, kindness of a grandmother.

Nameless Heroes

Only phenomena: sky covers, earth holds,
Four seasons move, oceans continue to widen ......
Like all the greatest, you have no names,
But actions and achievements.

You are recognized in all histories on
Victory, in the depths of all hearts.
You are respected sincerely, cleansed daily
By tears of gratitude, from which

Shines endless light, disclosing from above
That man has after all a bright future:
Those who build history are to be buried deep
In history, burnt to give warmth to newcomers.

You are the very life of history,
The very body of solemn humanity.
All the greatest have no names.
Those with names will be forgotten.

Nostalgia

The fine brush in lyrical dusk after the rain
Hesitates at the edge of a quiet river.
Water-flowers flow endlessly: a note from home.
Behind the bridge, the mountain at leisure is inkblue.

All walkers face a smiling rainbow, road
To home. Cattle, shaking now and then their bells, cross
Rivers. Sinking-floating homeward birds call.
Clouds, happy and bright, suddenly turn weeping.

A mother holding a child looks at a half moon
From water's broken edge. A lamp at the window
Comes through the water to me. In the barking
Of a dog who has caught a cold.
Tired and smiling, someone arrives home.

Season's Sorrowful Countenance

Sadly receiving, silently dripping, continually channelling,
The water bubbles under the eaves swirl and sink
Hastily gathered memories: those dead-stiff, groaning,

Yawning, backbending memories—their melancholic eyes
All turn toward me, begging me to sigh,
A sigh, a cold breath, grey like old lead roof-sheets.

Crowding, confusing rains drip-flow all over the surface,
And, like nibbling winds of winter, all thread and needle,
Pinch through my bones. Trees hang their heads.
Eyes, closing, closing, squeeze out several tears.
My heart, like a pond, has endless ripples
But can reflect nothing: A stretch of mushy mud in the battlefield.

(Written in war in India)

Fog

Its goal is to make us loners,
Make us vague with murkiness,
Turn people into prisoners, each locked
Inside white, doorless, windowless cells,
Change the city into mere houses, jungles
Into trees, rimless oceans into ponds . . . . . .

Not knowing that
As I was driven by severe cold and fatigue,
All curled inside frozen cotton, as it
Beseiges the outside walls of my small room,
Turning into a damp dark dungeon,
I can still see crowds from all directions,
Their steps, outcries, loudening ocean.

Trees amidst tempests wave up
Their angry arms, pliant grass-blades get
Ready to separate from earth to fly afar.
I see, too, evening silently carried away
By cooking smoke, by birds tired of flying.
In one short night, spring fields all at once
Put on the prettiest flowers and dews.

I have never seen this so dearly.
I have never felt this much satisfaction.

Language

I only believe in one simple language:
The language of fire, the strongest language.
The sun trusts it and sends on his
Kindness, his severity. Feeling uses it to carve
Charming pictures of the human world.

I generate heat. My tightened body is filled
With the brazen vocabulary of fire.
Through it, once for all, repressed thoughts
And emotions can find their fullest
Expressions, releasing the hidden strength of life.

I want to burn. A bonfire.
I am willing a cleanup destruction,
Leaving behind an illuminating memory,
Leaving behind a heap of iron-colored ashes.
At this moment, I only like radical language.

Only when we have convinced our enemies,
Crushing their citadels will we then
Cultivate Elegance, Elaborate Rituals,
Tastes and Leisure. But, for now,
I must use "barbarous" language.

Falling Leaves

Year after year, they fall, fall, generously swinging into every corner.
Year after year, they turn green, green hanging upon treetips,
Warming people's heart. No matter how many people
Lavish praises upon spring, delighted by new sprouts of
Tender green, when autumn comes, the same, curls and

Curls of them are scattered into ditches.
Just as a serious artist, always diligently, patiently
Waving his passionate hand, his hand guided by a
Sense of mission, writes and tears, tears and
Writes, writes, writes to no end, no, not until the
Most perfect, most satisfactory work is created.

Zheng Min (1920–)

Meeting at Night

I don't want to raise my hand to knock
For fear that the knock is too rousing.
There is a returning small boat,
No oars moved,
Waiting there for evening winds on the sea.
If you are sitting by the lamp
And hear the quiet breathing outside the door
And feel that someone is near who . . . . . .
Throws away his cigarette,
Noiselessly push open the door
You will find me, waiting there.

An Afternoon in Winter

The painter has gone to sleep,
Leaving the road lying colorless there.
Or is it meditating?
A pair of soft naked feet.
A checkered parasol.
Its face turns pale . . . . . .

The poplar complains, weeping:
"Where can we have beauty again?
Winds no longer eulogize me."
The crows are resting upon the stone-castle.
The sky is too low.

Loneliness drips from the branches.
I pass by a beauty asleep
Waiting for the breezes.
Someone lightly touches my elbow,
Pulls at my sleeves gently,
A pair of slightly tremulous small hands,
As if to whisper:
"No way of seeing her? . . . . . ."
So I stop and look back:
No travellers upon the road.

A lean branch of feeble white rose
Stretches outside the fence
Still trembling . . . . . .

Golden Sheaves

Golden sheaves stand
Upon the harvested fields of autumn.
I think of many tired mothers.
In the evening, on the road, I can see
Many beautiful wrinkled faces.
The full moon of harvest day is
In the dusk of the skyreaching
Branches. Distant mountains are
Skirting our heart.
No sculpture can compare with this silence.
Shouldering the great fatigue,
You, head-hanging, meditate in the autumn fields,
Stretching into a circle of distances,
Silent. Silent. History is but
A small river flowing away by our feet.
And you, standing there,
Will become a thought for mankind.

Music

Standing in the shadow of moonlight,
My soul is morning's flowing water.
Music flows out from your window,
But I do not know if your youthful life
Is running, in the same fashion, toward me?
But if we close our eyes,
Already we will be within the same realm,
Fish in the same river.

Sadness

Both of us are inside the same shadow,
Leaning upon the boat's railing, talking.
The autumn morning winds are indeed cold!
After a while as I am lowering my head,
Suddenly I seem to feel the sun touching my face.
O my cheeks are like thawing snow.
My heart is like warmed-up wine.
I raise my head and call to you:
Ah no! both of us are now inside the same sunlight?

Leaning upon the boat's railing, talking.
The autumn sun is truly warm!
Why do you merely smile, waving your hand?
Ah, one is on land, the other in the boat,
Which is moving slowly toward
That stretch of water under wide sunlight.

Renoir's Portrait of a Girl

Those who look for you enter the depths behind your eyelids,
Which, though half-opened, don't emit light to the world outside.
They are passages to the ocean of the soul, from where all your thoughts flow
Back into tranquil shapes as tides returning to the land.

Now I see your lips, so sternly closed,
Remind me of a pensive self locked among the rocky cliffs.
Though the richness of youth radiates from your lustrous hair,
You are yet so pale, resembling still a bleak spring.

Ah, you are not a star that emits light, neither
A fragrant rose, nor a fruit turned ripe,
But one enclosed before blossoming, bitter before maturity.

See how a soul first locks itself tight before it opens up
To the world; in deep meditation she gathers herself
In order to go towards a world that gives and takes love.

        (Translated by Leung Pingkwan)

Secret

The sky is like a thawing glacier,
When grey clouds crack open, pieces flying.
The grey clouds are like sails in a sea in tempests
In which birds fall and disappear from the sky of rolling clouds.
Suddenly, before this window, a corner of blue sky is offered,
As if from a chiseled ice-cave hole, one sees, for the first time,
The water which has been quietly flowing for a long time.
Upon the mirror-like sky is spring's shadow,
And on the tip of a tall evergreen tree,
The longish winter's melancholy is like a bird about to beat its wings.
Everything—from this confused orchestra finally comes a musical
   phrase:
A young man pushes open the window.
Like seeing a glowing white pagoda in the dream,
He raises up his whole soul,
But he is not with us;
He is listening: the distant sea, upon the mountains, in the very depth
   of earth.

Forest

This, too, is a symbol, symbol
Of millions of silent thoughts of the cosmos.
Not highrising like mountains,
Not brightening like the sea,
It stands still upon the earth's corner,
And locks within it with colors of gloom
A godsend, abundant.
Twisting-knotting branches, leaves lie above leaves.
In a depth not reachable by the eye,
The squirrels are meditating, leaves fall,
Light and shade float, new sprouts breathe,
And its form, as usual, remains silent,
Oblivious of the skyward eagle, travellers on the road,
Occasional winds and rains from the sea.
It neither speaks nor smiles, like a great great man.

A Village: Early Spring

I gaze at it:
It crouches at city's feet.
With a thousand sheets of darkbrown roofs,
And countless pieces of flying rags,
It depicts itself to the Universe,
Just as dwellers therein
Speak, paint, and cry out their lives
With their coarse skin.

Appreciating tongues would taste
From ripe fruits
A certain sweetness in life
Left behind by trees
After persevering winters
Confounding springs, tempestuous summers.
A sympathetic mind
Sees through the smiling village in the sun
To every single dark night after long rain

When thatched roofs tremble
Walls waver
To protect some people.
Poverty behind them
Now transforms itself into
A fierce dog in the woods . . . . . .
But look, how it now proudly opens its bosom
Like a well in high heat summer, sharing its
Water to passers-by.
It spreads out a soft scene for
Those unjustly taken to be stupid and clumsy,
For those muddy feet, fatigued shoulders,
Haggard faces and neglected lonely hearts.
How now women are washing clothes, children at play
Dogs running, light smoke rise to the sky.
Most resembling the thawing river is the unlocked happiness after a long term
Which begins to flow slowly when suddenly they spot,
Adding onto tree tips every night,
Banners of green hope.

Loneliness

This dwarf palm tree—
Has it been standing here
All year long
Before my door?
I seem to have returned from a boisterous banquet.
When the afterglow from the sky
Hits it standing by itself
In the green sheen of earth and moss,
I suddenly fall back into the world,
Into its very depth,
Where, I feel,
It quietly closes in my surrounding,
Like a sinking mud pond.
My eyes open, as it were,
In the deep, dark night,

And see clearly all things
In their most secret moments.
My ears
Wake up suddenly
And hear all things
Speaking in the evening:
I face the world alone.
I am lonely.
When the white day is dissolved by darkness,
I sit before my door.
Outside the house now, in half-sky,
Are flying those
Disappearing laughs.
In the distance, some people
Are promenading along the river,
As I see:
Swallows pecking along the bosom of the water,
A large tree of early spring
About to cover the river.

I remember two rocks in the sea.
Some say that they are not lonely.
They sun together.
They splash up white waves together.
They guard the silence of the sea together.
But to me, they are
But two big trees rooted in the courtyard,
Unable to walk.
Even though they are arm in arm,
Hair in hair,
They are but two latticed squares
Upon a glass window,
Always locked in position.
O how men
Yearn for a mixed life:
This body within that body!
This soul within that soul!

In this world, where is the dream
That we can dream together with another person?
We climb up snow-capped mountains together.
We promenade along the river together.
But who can put one
Into the other's body,
Friend, lover,
Person locked in oaths,
Together
To listen to words told to oneself alone by life,
To see the countenance revealed to oneself alone by life,
To feel what is felt:
Fear, suffering, hope, happiness?
In my heart, there are
Many starlights and shadows,
That nobody can see.
When my love and I took a walk,
I saw many devils and angels,
I smelt many scents of early spring,
I saw a raincloud flying here.
That moment, I heard the joys of orioles.
That moment, I heard turtledoves presaging rain.
But because people live their lives —
Each to himself.
I am reminded of
One rock, another rock,
One tree, another tree,
A dream unparticipatible.

Why do I always hope
To stay close to a huge tree like a vine?
Why do I always feel
Being pushed into a crowd of strangers?
I always pray:
Come, let us unite together,
Not to go play,
Not to go walk;
What I want to say is: Do you see

The heavy rain that is coming to my heart?
When loneliness comes close to me,
The world brusquely, relentlessly,
Walks straight into my bosom,
I quietly watch the full cedar tree, thinking:
Would it open its full round body,
Its complete world,
And let me walk into it, taking it as a haven?
But one day when I feel
"Loneliness" bites my heart like a snake,
Suddenly, I know:
I am together
With a most faithful companion.
When the whole world of men turn away their faces,
When the entire mankind who cannot listen hear my greetings,
It will always stay close to my heart.
It allows me to see, within some silent light,
Every part of the world;
It allows me to have a pair of aerial eyes
To find this "me" sitting inside the house with
All her emotions, all her thoughts.
When I am a child of toys,
When I am a youth in love,
I am always lonely.
We walk together many roads
Until eventually we see
"Death" in the half-light of dusk,
Wearing his long gown.
Why not take back these laughable, anticipating eyes
From trees and rocks,
They are dumb, deaf, incommunicable.
I think of people who, from pains of fire,
Get the last rest of being "pious".
I, too, will, from the bites of "loneliness"
Seek out the most serious meaning of "life".
Because of it, be it
Violent snow-storms of winter, be it
Raging waves in oceans,

People never stop struggling.
Come, my tears,
My painful heart
I am happy to know where
It tears at and oppresses my heart.
I throw away all the ridiculous smallness, pettiness
Of man into its rimlessness
And see them:
Life is after all a torrential river.

                    1943 Kunming

Chen Jingrong (1917–1989)

Phenomena

Rivers
Lines and lines
Crisscross upon the ground
Streets
Stretches and stretches
Cross and connect one another

Not one blade of grass
Can boast of being alone
Not one single syllable
Can become language

Arms and arms
Connect in the night
Eyes in pairs
Look toward tomorrow

4/2/46 Chungking

Poems of No Tears

> A true man does not shed tears easily
> Only because he is not yet caught in distress.
> —"Lin Chong Fleeing at Night"

Countless windows open and close.
Misty fine rains
Pull late spring into autumn.
Elegies on autumn by ancient poets

Are now all quiet, cold.
Giant flags flutter.
Where the wind blows, a sweep of blood-stench.

After roving all over the world,
Treading every road,
Who can still raise
His foot but lightly
And flick away
Indifferently the soil stuck in the sole?

Tears over a stage story.
All quiet now, drums and gongs upstage.
All grief-stricken still, audience downstage.
On the streets, blurring dusk deepens.
Old beggars bow their heads upon the ground,
Hitting it louder and louder.

Strange indeed! Of what generation is this spring?
Of what nationals is this foreign country?
      May 9, 1947
      Shanghai

Ships and Us

In the busy harbor,
Ships and ships
Take different directions.

In busy streets people indifferently pass,
Indifferently kick up dust,
Let voices, sounds converge into a hubbub.
People come, people go,
Each holding his own destiny.

But in tempestuous seas,
Ships beckon other ships,
When coincidentally they meet.

In deserted mountains or islands,
People's ears anxiously
Wait for words from strangers.

                    Chungking 1945.6.21

Sallow Dusk, I am at Your Side

Sallow Dusk, I am at your side.
Because I am at the window's side,
I am, thus, like a silhouette
Stuck against far-reaching pale yellow.

Day is to leave and is not leaving.
Night is to come and is not coming.
Hung in this haziness between half-light and half-dark,
I and rows and rows of blankly staring roofs.

Streetlamps begin to glimmer.
The city is preparing a colorful wakeup.
Don't just stand there under the lightpoles,
Wander, listen, listen to:
Music—if this is music—
Shrill shrieks of a hundred degrees tremble
Embrace the suffocating city,
Laughing wickedly.

Hiding into a long, long quiet street,
Sallow Dusk, I now find your tender hand
Holding mine, like an old friend,
Amidst the loss, I turn back
As you begin to tell me
Some very very old stories,
Stories that have already sallowed in my memories,
Sallowed like your face—
With a stroke of afterglow in the distant sky.

In the stories, there are grandfather's whitebeards,
Mother's embroidered skirt,
Cobble-stoned streets of my native town,
And the unusual bright mood amidst dogs barking.

There are snowstorms of the north,
The iciness of the Pass,
Homeward dreams of years and months,
The cold sun of the million-mile Yellow River.

Ai, East, West, North, South, I am but
An invisible black dot.
People say: from airplanes, mountains and rivers
Are like toy building blocks,
And people, to and fro upon the earth,
Are ants crawling upon a mere ball.

Sallow Dusk, alas, with your stories,
I have become silent.

Silent, because dark night is coming,
Because, for no reason, griefs and fears.
No wind, yet leaves drop one by one,
Throwing upon our shoulders strange coldness.

Sallow Dusk, I made a detour
And come back to your side.
Now I hear dark night beating its wings.
I want to climb upon it, to fly, to fly,
Until, all beaten, I drop down by night's side.
There will be dawning,
There will be the gorgeous morning sun.

      Shanghai 1946.10.26

A Logic Patient's Spring

I

Water running too fast
Appears not to run.
Wheels running too fast
Appear not to turn.
A face with over-laughing
Appears to be weeping.
In light too bright
You see nothing
As in the dark.

Perfection is imperfection.
Fullness is emptiness.
Greatest is smallest.
Zero is infinity.

Oldest of the old, this world
Seems to be forever fresh.
Whatever things from grandma's chests and trunks
Would easily make a new boutique.

II

Too many forms, gestures, signs and sounds
We are now tired of! Ai!
You never seem to get old, you, blue sky!
In a warm spring morning
Bombers are circling in the sunlight.

Nature is a huge hospital;
Spring, a doctor; sunlight, medicine,
To wake up the beaten soul,
To revive the withering trees.

We have a thousand counts of ennui.
Days are relentlessly pushed up our spine.
Since spring is here, perhaps we can
Stretch ourselves and yawn a couple of times.

Even though there is rimless green in our imagination,
Yet water, O, water, water,
We are still longing in
Unending thirst.

III

Living in life.
Work. Food. Sleep.
Laugh for a reason. Cry for a reason.
Nothing seems to be out of order.

Turtle-doves whine in a fine day,
Calling for winds, calling for rains—
What is sad is that hope
Dies of thirst in desperation.

Build up the citadel of will,
And then pace back and forth.
You forgive
And hate yourself.

IV

Suddenly there is a raging gale in the dream
Mixed with dogs' barking everywhere.
Winds stop. Whose door,
Whose heavy door is so heavily shut?
As if it were me, and me alone,
That had been locked out of sleep,
Listening by myself
The rumbling of a speedy train.

O the cold currents
Of Siberia are long gone—

Then, you ask, is this the true
Spring? Yes, do you not see
That sunlight has begun to feel soft,
That willows are dangling in tendrils,
That the earth has grown green hair,
And that even winds are drunk?

We only wait for thunders.
Thunders, the first series of spring's thunders
Will wake up the insects' sleep.
These will be real thunders, mind you,
And not just the cold-ridden coughs
Of the sky.

Children's Day: a few lucky ones
Are brightly dressed in a celebration,
Saluting, making speeches, receiving awards.
Meanwhile, countless young laborers are in factories,
Whose health is slowly being wrecked by
Eight to ten hours of hard work.

Cheating and lying, twins from the same stem.
Spring, we know you have plenty of
Short-lived flowers!
Memorial day: heart-smiting horns are blown.
We are living: no time
To let loose a flood of tears.

Small sardines.
In the modern city, we are being
Squeezed, as usual. Squeezed,
All four basics of life—
Clothing, food, housing, transportation—
Squeezed every way, and only squeezing can give you room.

Birds, beasts, insects, fishes can never
Get their share of our concern.
Sorrow, joy, separation, reunion—
These are too common.
Everything is "squeezed" out into exile,
Leaving here a big BLANK.

No sorrow from last night's dream to this morning.
Mountains and rivers: In the dream we have lost the bridges.
Tomb-sweeping Day and Mid-Autumn Festival*,
In no way can they command winds, rains, or moon.

There is always something to say, something to do.
A new beginning always follows an ending.
Once you stop, willing or not,
This is death.
Shanghai, April, 1947.

---

* Tomb-sweeping Day, or Qing-ming Day, almost always falls on a rainy day, as made famous by this line of classical Chinese poetry: "In Qing-ming Day, drizzles blown about in confused lines of silk." Mid-Autumn Festival celebrates the 15th night of the Eighth Moon when the moon is supposed to be the biggest, roundest, and brightest.

Hang Yuehe (1917–)

Serious Game

With a rifle, a sabre, a red-tasseled spear,
You bare enemies' corpses by their side.
With a mountain slope, a stretch of forest,
You stop the enemies' chase, cutting their retreat.

War is like a game: a thousand times, a million times,
Breaking wholes into parts, parts into wholes. Today,
In the serious game, it has grown into
An earth-shaking, direction-controlling strength.

"Wipe them out!" And so, your weapons succeed in
Equipping them, your fate rolled into their hands.
Outrage, howling, driving divisions of lives into war—
Changed into smoke, into ash, into their friends.

From surfaces to lines, lines to dots, concentrate,
Concentrate! Design afresh strategies and techniques.
In the past, you belittle their every little bit,
Now they launch a campaign, plundering, looting.

Common sense and history give you revelations:
Breed fish on dry land. This stake to bet
Is strangely new. Moths yearn for fire, burnt by fire.
You, too, seem to have this courage to receive?

February 1948
Shanghai

Intellectuals

Yearning for the world of the past,
You peruse books and books of famous biographies,
By a slant of moonlight, a bottle of fireflies,
Inside the wall, a silk cap is laid aside.

A mirror hung before the nose,
You go out to the market to buy a horoscope,
Who would be restful with this simple tea and rice?
Take off a commoner's clothes, clamber up the skies.

Tons of lofty projects are buried in books.
Histories of a million years will never lie.
But now you have lost your teeth, hair all white,
And autumn leaves cover the road before the door.

This old long gown has been dragging on.
You: Half an empty life at your study's window.

December 1946
Shanghai

Last Performance

You want us to express our joy with fire-crackers.
You want us to celebrate by hanging flags.
You want us to raise our hands to hurrah for you.
Smiling, you play this last masterpiece.

Memory and reason are a pair of twins
We have learned to forget,
To swallow the blood lesson, and ten years' tears.
Holding you, we support a struggle of life and death.

Ever since you rebel against human nature and your promises,
The old scars begin to bloom again in our hearts.
Your coveted desire you can only finish half.
This monotonous farce: The cast you hastily put together.

Escort you to up the stage! What a cast! What a Program!
Firecrackers, flags, hurrahs, you know,
Cannot stop the winds and rains from around,
Laughing convulsedly, laughing tremblingly, you know.

We are an audience led here by a string
To watch, with eyes all bloodshot,
Your last performance. Millions of
Howls and applauses, waiting for our call.

> May 1948
> Shanghai

Revelation

We often find ourselves lost in our own small world.
Picking up a shell or catching a green worm
Would bring us some elation, as if
This world already belongs to us, and we are
Locked inside a ball of mist;
Turning or leaping, we end up inside a palm.

We woke up suddenly one day,
Our beard and hair all burnt.
From the fish in the water, and the birds in the sky,
We got a revelation. So
We crossed waters, crossed mountains,
Throwing away the mirror that we loved
And began to seek a world outside our world.

A blade of grass from roadside stone crevices,
A pool of spring off the cliff, and
Also small animals jumping around,
Told us a history,
And taught us how to try ourselves
From this point to the next point.

Today, we would not sigh so easily—
A flower's decay, a moon's waning.
A star's fall, an egg-shell's breaking.
Will all presage some life's anxieties

Coming to us, all will point out for us
The road ahead,
Because the changes of their lives
Have smoothed out so many of life's ups and downs,
To lead us to a new world
—a world beyond our own world.

June 1947
Shanghai

Prelude

Often we try to catch an ideal; we are
Sometimes caught by it, and are kept
In a bottomless nightmare, adrift
Between the crisscrossing of nights and days.

O long long days, with outcries
And weeping, are distilled through our living:
Thunderlike rumbling, lightning-like flashes,
Flood-like spurt out of the ground.

We raise together our trembling hands, to snatch MAN's
Position, to fill up the body-shell empty for years.
Thenceforth, there will always be people where

We will find mountains, rivers, houses, For this song-bereft nation,
Let us compose new tunes with color-brushes
And tell the children the birth of this fairy-tale.

Shanghai, 1948
from *Resurrected Earth* (Shanghai, 1949)

From "Gluttonous Sea" in *Resurrected Earth*

II

Let us break out from this suffocating,
Nightmare-filled
    illusive house,
Leaving the trickery of words
Behind doors. We go
Onto the streets, onto the streets . . . . . .

Streets where gutters churn
With heat-currents: no sunlight. People,
Like fermented dead water, steaming,
From each door, port of each house,
Pour out, flooding the wide yet narrow
Boulevards.
    Tall buildings—petrified
Giants rise up from all the roofs,
Causing our hats to fall, our burning desire to rise,
To discover that man is but a small, pitiable
Ant: Day in, day out, wheels roll over,
Rolling away lives; frozen lives
Under humid eaves; fainted
Lives upon bustling
Pavements; lost lives inside
Darkly-guarded prisons . . . But, this is
Shanghai— flower of the cosmopolitan:
People come here, following
Various dreams with wisdom and labor,
Come here, a pile of garbage, now a
Paradise.
    We go onto the streets.
We swim in the Milky Way of the Paradise.
O listen, this is the celestial music. This is
Music? Which causes our ear-drum to swell,
Our breathing, hard-pressed, the loudening
Surge of people, between them, no crevices.
Trembling of malaria, motors, horns, shrill

And sharp in unison . . .
Stop! Black police cars, white
Ambulances, red fire-engines brush by
The commas of our barely-stopped feet; they
Row by, fly by, howl by
So violent is the shrill cry that every speck of dust
Would tremble . . . This is no music,
(Or perhaps this is?) music which
Fills everywhere, in full speed,
In the highest intensity, to race about,
To entice, to ransack. We are ants,
Or fish. We bathe
In the currents of music. Listen! Listen!

> There, flowers open, bloom after bloom,
> And you do not pluck.
> Here, buds are waiting to bloom,
> You fly over for luck.

Fly over! Fly over! Too many
Sirens are turned into canaries in show windows
Of every house, enticing colorful visitors
To sink into sleep beside them. The colors of seasons
Are changed by their changes. Listen!

> Y　IY　IY　IY　IY　IY The loved one.
> Once gone, no news. Y　IY　IY　IY　IY
> IY　　My heart is broken.

Listen! O This is again music. This is
Music? O This is music's prison.
This note enfolds a number of ears, and
That note enfolds a series of laughs.
Escape! We go through circles of notes.
We have lost our voice. Would that
This loss leads to that of the notes!
Escape! Escape from a horde of hunger-ridden,
Licentious beasts, and pass over, pass

Over the torture of this music . . .
    O torture of music!
The temptation of a terrifying devil, tormenting
Our hearing, tormenting
Two lips swept by sunset.
Growing up from the same mire, we are
Subject to a malicious scheme, which, spitting out
Blood-lines, spreads yellow
Anaesthetics, and puts this land under
Its domination. Following its own corruption,
Conscience—A million good hearts—is worm-eaten.

O my God, if you had given us
A naked heart, please give us now
A clean, naked world.

III (in part)

This is Shanghai—sister of New York, London,
Paris. Look! Overtaking us
In striding fashion are those aliens,
Brown hair, green eyes, once
Masters here. We followed them and
Turned with them on a gray sand road, and
Learned to be "gentlemen" under their
Conductor's rod, in a dark room,
And thus: the following outrageous signboard must be taken down

   CHINESE AND DOGS ARE NOT ALLOWED!

Today, we want to come back as masters here . . . .

Tang Qi (1920–1990)

Fog

I

Greywhite fog
Walks, in the night,
With its clumsy huge polar bear steps.

Lower, wetter, dirtier
Than clouds, it walks and squats down
With its weightless
Boundless white buttocks.

Slowly, slowly
It rises—
And moves toward still lower lands.

II

It has forgotten those quiet
Mountains, forests, crisscross highways,
And thatched houses close together behind it.
It alone can raise up
An infinite sky-screen
To cover the sober eyes of men
And make everything feebler, vaguer
With its bad breaths.

The city suddenly becomes grey and down,
Like a slum without thickness,
Upon darkened streets, misty, humid.

Dusk is paralyzed
In people's short-sightedness.
In the vague spreading fog, no more
Space, but a few unclear standing shadows.
Upon the wharf, among the heldup cargoes
Are found only filthy mice,
Those despicable small grey animals! . . .

Ferries call, estranged:
Night speeds up Time, the hypnotized
Big clock of the River is almost asleep.
Streetlamps, however, are thinking of distant things,
Of wanderers with too much bodily freedom, now detained
Inside prisons of no thick white walls.
Roofs and roofs are slowly disappearing.
Fog becomes bigger;
Only it knows itself.

III

It makes those imprisoned
In dark rooms— reporters, intellectuals,
Students— stroke their heads, sighing,
Hands holding undeliverable news . . .

It spies at the only lighted
Window, where an innocent sleepless girl yawns,
Where issues a lamplike solitude with eyes wide open
Toward the nightmare world.

It guards attentively, however,
Like a group of white secret police,
Shielding around an isolated tall house,
Those schemers, strategists, armsmongers,
Who, using peace as a white smokescreen,
Draw and chart, with bones of men,
Every square foot of their territory,
Dominating we don't know how much flesh and blood

Signs that assemble death.
They grin hideously, feigning ignorance . . .

IV

O Fog is spreading, giving cover to
The endless rains behind its heels.
The people need explore no more:
Under the grey peace, darkly,
A stretch of war's quagmire.

1947
Chungking

From *Time and Banner*

I

Hear the bell?
Vibrating in light, vibrating in darkness, clinging
Before and behind this space,
It takes days away, takes nights away; not a fiction
Of forms, but look! in a stretch of thin light,
Day alternates with night. Standing on the Heights in central
  Shanghai,
Time in a society, semi-feudal, semi-colonial, scatters down
A handful of needles toward a sea of people.
Outside life, who controls
House and house, window and window?
The deepest contemplation of the spiritual is like a sorrowful hand.

Men have endured too much reality,
Often not sensing out immediately its meaning.
In the cold wind, hopes, blown away
One by one, wither like gorgeous flowers, and like sheets of paper,
Are torn and blown back: it is always
Time echoing the bell's oblivion.
Past time stays here, and here is
Not completely past. The present swells within,
And it is the future, always, that comprehends all

The joys and separations, conspiracies and needs of assistance.
Verdicts are being made upon countless consciences
By a power, despicable and mean.

Hopes deep in eyes, and hearts constantly
Inter-weave inside and outside life, we endure,
Like the breeding of starfish, the incubation of birds,
Many failures. Through the morning streets, and
Among the crowds, we discover our own existence.
The sun has not been wrested from us,
Although the sky is spread with dense rainclouds.
What coldness, how full of evils, this world!
People seem to have been returning from the eclipse.

Endless endurance is a flame—
Behind layers of barbed-wires of factories,
By the gloomy barred windows of Tilan Bridge Prison,
In the slums covered by severe frosts,
In the black-awning boats carrying conscript peasants,
Beside the bamboo-chairs of shops where young girls are sold,
Inside the blank pupils of those starved to death by the Suzhou River,
In street corners enveloped by a huge shadow,
The fires of hunger and protests are scorching too many of us.
People are waiting silently between ice and flames,
O, the fire-fetcher is coming in the dark.
. . . .
. . . .

II

In mid-April still cold in the South,
I walk toward the Shanghai Heights awash in golden sunset.
Still under the sycamore leaves in the Concession,
Next to the Jewish Hatong Park,
My words echo in the minds of
Many individuals and startle clusters of flowers
Dangling in the Park. Coming depressions, laden distresses,
All not to be questioned openly—

I can do nothing but point toward
Time. The hollow time of the capitalists
Inches on, trembling, presaging inevitable dissolution.
Here, all the carts and hubs
That rolled over disclose not their orbits, their curves.
Beyond train windows are
Green grains in the fields, but no birds to eat them.
Peasants escape from the ripening green
And other worries, hidden fears in the heart
Are like shafts of rain in ambush. In the Season of Plenty,
More people are starved . . . . . .
    Far and near, we can still see
Neck-twisted chimneys from roofs
Of mud houses, no cooking smoke in the evening
To presage happiness. From the cracks of thatched huts,
Winds return; no salt in ceramic jugs.
Eyes are now two pieces of ice held by
A melancholic plate-like face since the frost of winter solstice.
Under some dried leafless trees,
Pitiful deaths will soon be dissolved.
In the shivering autumn, words in the wind:
Whose land is this after all? Whose fields?
Tenant farmers know too well their green
Memories. From the huts that contain darkness of their years,
They now must depart,
Because of the increasing burden
Imposed upon them
By the insatiable warring government.
Peasants, taken as an old, bent,
Feudal measurement, labor upon fields and fields,
Adapting themselves to all sorts of landlords. They are driven
Outside the city walls
To wait, patiently, each in his own fears.
O quiet earth, land that is not vacant,
Peasants lose their sorghum-red blood
Into it. They are used to
Life being turned into mud; long-term
Offer is but this body exhausted by poverty.

...... O shivering autumn.
Women are at their spinning-wheels, shaking autumn
In October. The bleak singing of crickets
Stops. Day and night turn against each other
In a stretch of thin light. The heart-splitting story is
The continuous weeping at windows. Children in hunger
Dare not walk close to the gardens
Of landlords, or to venture into the city.
They sit down between white poplars and tombs,
In the potato-fields, like a plough,
Like a new-born calf, totally unaware of
Fate. The farming techniques of serfdom
Remain here from the long long past,
Between ice and flames, in the dimming sunlight at year's end,
All quietly buried with the white snow.

IV

Deserted, chilling monthend. I walk
Toward the Shanghai Heights bathed in golden sun, a dazzling
Place occupied by capitalists and machines
Beneath the dark crystal marble buildings, all
Mirror-smooth, coolies in large numbers are pushing loaded carts.
The blending basses and tenors of men and women
Dissolves into a huge dustless clamor ......
....
Under the illusive flower mis-matched by
The moon and neonlights, day and sky are gone.
High-speed trams are busily running.
In the end, falsehood and exaggeration have let
People focus on wealth and rank, glittering
Names in the graveyard, and colorful red poppies.
With variegated roots planted in the sewers,
They stretch out their black hands, and, aided by
Relations and relations, support, campaign for,
And squander into all forms of corruption.
From the empty trembling of the wireless that runs
From the highest buildings along grey walls,

Bustling people tightly hold onto a thin
Coldness, like sheets of cellophane in the wintry wind.
Before the eyes, a smutty Suzhou River flows across the heart.

Children are not startled. Upon the masts
Of the newest warships anchored all over the harbor,
Star-shaped flags are flashing, vigilantly watching
The way they watched the colonies of Africa.
One wire in the networking of the war-monger
Upon Pacific Bases has now reached here . . . . . .

Go back to that garden:
People adore exotic bouquets.
Women put on gorgeous dresses and
Faces, their arms held by strutting gentlemen.
They had too many dark yesterdays
Reflected upon the Sunday sunlight.
Across the sheen of the pool, a bird
Flies past. Such is the instant: Trees meditate;
People crowd toward the Garden gate;
A black cat jumps out of the green mansion,
So bright is the sun at noon,
So dizzily bright, all forms, void of ideals,
Void all your thoughts.

And countless sick people lie lethargic
By the railway stations. Unhoused alien accents
Upon the main street suffer from pains of deformities
And oppressive acts. Life is no life,
Souls all stilled. Under a long line
Of light poles in the evening, endless disclosures
With darkness crowded here, helpless, tell:
Day in day out we are
Covered by shadows behind "fences of death,"
Which, enraging us, will turn us into
Relentless bombs; inactive gunpowder,
Detonated, will take revenge upon them.

By the side of the garden
Lawns outside the traffic zone
Are many musical houses, balconies and windows
With Jews, Englishmen and armored
American troops and marines patrolling
Their "hometown" upon the "colony".
The hymns from the international Cathedral
Wash clean their sins.
But like an unlighted bathroom hiding dirts,
Jewelled and flowered ladies and their hybrid
Dogs walk whimsically in their desires.
Time has not made them learn to forgive
And forget. Fumbling with lies, lustful hands hold still
The last golden key which locks and unlocks
Wealth and buildings, inflowing, outflowing
Exact gold coins, and exquisite commodities
Filling this entire idiotic colony.
The pendulum in the clock of the Customs House
Swings between exploitation and conspiracy.
Counting wealth every minute
Ready to be shipped back at the last hour
To their home country, aware of
That inevitable end that is to come—
Wealth is not wealth;
No occupation will persist.
Armaments cannot forever protect a colony.
The silent people are saturated with fury.
A contract made by only a few is history to be cursed.
A new Time belonging to us will soon order
Their simple and quick demise.

VI

Look! The winds of war!
The arrival of startling tempests is daily quickened.
They have awakened bare winter trees and
Seeds beneath the earth. People in the tempests,
Awakened, will give themselves to fighting.

With this,
We will laugh loudly, opening mouths unopened for centuries.
With the winds, a thousand years of brutality and despotic acts
Will be cracked in one decisive moment.
All the land will change. The strongest flames will rise from blood
To shine over glorious life and death.

VII

Struggling will change all meanings
In this huge process, future will unfold the cruel
Yet benevolent Time, completed
In the banner of the people.

VIII
Through the winds, people will gradually see
A new land: Flowers bloom, birds sing,
Mankind dawns anew.
From the conquest by labor, and the awakening in war,
We will hold upon a Time:
People might still suffer,
But winds of festivity and happiness will soon blow.

Past time stays here, and here is
Not completely past. The present swells within,
And it is the future that comprehends a consistent
Direction. A huge historical image is completed
In this banner of the people, shining
Like the sun, brightening before and behind this space,
From here to there.

       Shanghai, 1948

Tang Shi (1920–)

The Girl Who Steals Ears of Wheat

Earth, your skin.
Wheat awn, your hair.
Your hands, withered branches.
Inside your palms, wrinkles of bark.

You hastily walked through paths in the fields
Like mole-rats jumping across furrows.
Inside your eyes, a dusking sun.
Inside your pupils, flooding light of confidence.

Like a hen searching the harvested field,
Picking up buried grains one by one,
You cocked your ears on the ground,
Waiting footfalls to fade upon the paths.

And furtively ran to the fields, plucked ears of wheat,
And hid them in your bosom, hiding a whole heart of joy.
Wind blows your fluttering neckerchief
The way night blows its light whistle.

1946

Sing to Future

Let people who sleep sleep soundly.
Let those in whose eyes is found lips' thirst,
And those in whose brains is found stomach's hunger sleep soundly.
Before the blue blue sky
I will bury my eyes in endless wild grass.

Misty-mazy grass is like ancient jungles,
Long dense summer, no beginning, no decline.
Everything sings toward a complete future.

Let people who sleep sleep deeply.
Let those in whose eyes is found lips' thirst,
And those in whose brains is found stomach's hunger sleep deeply.
Inside my heart is a purple cloud
With love conceiving hate, with hate moving toward love.
Nature will emerge with seasonal clothes,
As Pleistocene reptiles will wake up from thunder,
Startle not by a myriad things' tenderness, whole, sublime love.

Poetry

Only when pounding tides recede
Can the beach offer its bright, bright shells.
If poetry is to take root in life's soil,
It should emerge in life's victory.

Fruits come in the wake of falling flowers.
Only after glittering days can we have pregnant nights.
If man can live at the edge of day and night
In the thin light there will be a new mixing.

A whole day of sun ends vertically with the horizon.
The grey dove-bells are coming closer and closer.
O in difficult times I pray that a thundering fire
Will scorch *this me*, will scorch *that me*.

Four sides close up, three corners wedge in.
Beyond oneself, I welcome another self.

Rodin

When life's drifting gestures
Suddenly congeal in a firm white marble,
When citizens' continually extending hands

Suddenly congeal in a stretch of fearless love,
Rodin, it is you who said to us:
Sacrifice is a glorious tragedy; for love,
A fountain spurts out transparent beads,
An umbrella, scattering a strangely colorful light.

Quietly, you gather the strength of the mind
To explore each wrinkle upon the forehead,
To explore the birth of each thought,
To let the body, the limbs confluent with veins,
Continually spurt out a young, joyful spring.

In an immeasurable luminosity, what new
World are you exploring?
Let the first one who thinks deeply
With a full body of rich sinews
And blood running silently upon the forehead
Lay his foot upon a universe, complete, immense, sublime.

For Fang Qi

We met in each other's
Misfortunes. Our manacles
Rang aloud our solitude.
How strange indeed our intimate
Days! Insults had become
The solid ground we shared.

Twenty-four hours every day we faced
Ourselves, faced tall walls.
Your heart was the mirror of
My selfishness, reflecting mountains, waters
Of the past, of the coming
Days, and firmer, stronger nights.

From the hand's hold came
Tenderness. In silence, one contained
A bigger world, respecting all

Sincere sacrifices. Tears, grief, you
Returned from the torture room.
"Why can't man be firmer, braver?"

"I should not be the one to sacrifice."
You hated your own eyes and mouth,
Because they had disclosed your
Illusive cleverness. Thus, you
Became silent up in the tempestuous tower,
Breathed the power of knowledge
From beyond the ocean, and felt the

Humidity of the times. Greedily you
Opened your sincere heart, to plant
A stubborn life. You busied about
In the new festive days
Of the future. In the morning, you burned
A little intimate flame . . . . . .

Now, under the sun, strangely
Lost is your shadow, you have
Again accepted another silent trip.

The Tumultuous City

Petroleum tanks, children are pulling you
Like pulling sharp ploughs,
Ploughing through the streets, ploughing through the heart of the
    city,
Ploughing on the shoulders of people.

Businesses close down, clamor rises,
Strike, the tall buildings of the city tremble.

Pale yellow night, street lamps are extinguished,
Eyes of the city are extinguished,
Pulse of the city stops,
People in shadowy shapes, like tides,

Rush over
    Rush back.
A gust of wind sweeps off the floating light of the city.
The whirling wind rolls forward like wolves.
Shop windows—noses of the city
That smell—stuffed.
All fragrance and colors, all temptations of the city,
Are blown away by the wind.
In the theatre, the applauding ladies and gentlemen
Steal away like cats,
Leaving the embarrassed, white-nose clown
In ridiculous multi-colored clothes
Standing on the dark and empty stage.

Prices rush out of the chimney
Soaring like black smoke into the sky.
Sound of the petroleum tanks
Sow the undying seeds.
This city would never calm down.
O tumultuous city, turpid city!
The plough of life drags the gait of everyone,
Rushing towards the heart of the city.

(Translated by Leung Pingkwan)

Yuan Kejia (1921-)

Nanking

One dream: thirty years, waking up to hostile eyes.
In great confusion, one forgets the true energy is oneself.
Flying all over the sky are pretidal red dragonflies,
Blaming and blaming, always blaming others: the third stage of inferiority complex.

Thinking that if you held a high-voltage line,
Now happy, now angry, you could control the world.
To flatten you, people all around have taken to cheat.
The uncheating ones, you name them reactionaries, rebels.

Officials all over, meetings, meetings, paid.
Disorder is yourself; spears toward others; hand holds Telefuken,
Promulgating to rebels in four directions: All four, emptiness.

The muddle-headed feel heartaches in seeing you.
The analysts simply call you schizophrenic.
Washington reaches into the money bag: a bottomless hole!

Shanghai

Ask not how many people have predicted its demise,
That every year it will sink a few inches.
New buildings reach up still, like devil's arms,
Pillaging earth's sunlight, earth's moisture,

Ghost shadows all over. Greed goes on up in high skies.
A desperate battle starts all telephones ringing.
Numbers inside windows are mixed-up nerves.
Spread upon the ground, empty eyes of hunger.

Uneven everywhere. And yet days pass easily
From offices to bars, one straight-line track:
Make money for ten hours, make love for ten hours.

Gentlemen walk in with bulging pot-bellies
Met by pink yawns of typists who would cover
Their faces with newspapers: wait for rumors from Nanking.
                              1940

The Times: Some Thoughts

Why do you hump over your desk writing at this time still,
When royalties earned cannot earn you the writing paper sent out,
When nobody really cares about what you have to say,
Who asks, instead, what flag you wave and shout for,
When the talent of dissenters becomes unforgiven sin,
Whereas picking up spittles of comrades is like picking up pearls?

Why do you still bury yourself in reading at this time,
When intellectuals band together to curse knowledge,
When students suspect that all books contain poison,
That the teachers between blackboards and them are doomed
   bookworms,
When, shunning books, foreign and traditional, like poisonous gas,
They are forced to swallow in doses the empty "heavenly text"?

Because what beseiges us is unprecedented humiliation,
The center of culture daily announcing the death of learning.
Amidst this pervasive sinking somebody has to rise up
To crush the superstition that folly is all holy,

And break through the black hell that is closing upon us,
And hold a little light to wait for the dawn after the holocaust.
1948

Heavy Bell

Leave me silent in Time and Space,
Like a rustgreen bell in an ancient temple,
Carrying three thousand years of weight,
To hear hurrying tempests outside the window.

Throw waves back to the ocean.
Return infinity to the blue sky.
I am a soundless bell,
Soundless like the frozen blue.

Life fruits from miseries,
Miseries baked by dead silence,
I am a rustgreen bell
To receive wild winds from all over.
1946

Nearing You

Only nearing you do I notice the true distance of the scale.
The traveller moves his steps from a map back to land.
Rising like a tall tower, you command a tradition of solitude.
Seeing you, the "strait" suddenly understand widening distances.

The fullness of virgin forests, the steaming dark of tropical nights.
Tonight, I have nothing to abandon; Being is everything.
Scorching, firm, like dealing with enemies who respect order,
You move into positions more certain and clearer than constellations.

Charting out counter positions, one creates reality.
Between stars, an endless expanse, transparent, dynamic;
I swell up like a mountain range against the clear, clean space,
To be exorcized by the blue, to receive again training.

Your prayer standing up: Not to receive, not to reject,
A complete mellow independent whole: "I am reality".
Gazing at the distance is like gazing at tragedy—
Romantically beautiful, you decide to devote yourself to miracles.

                              1947

Lu Yuan (1922–)

When I Was A Small Child

When I was a small child,
I could not read.
Mom was my library.

I read Mom—

One day,
Peace rules the world.
People can fly . . .
Wheat comes out of snow . . .
Money becomes useless . . .

Gold pieces are used as bricks for houses,
Banknotes as paper for kites,
Coins as plates thrown to drift across water surfaces.

I want to be a wandering youth,
Bringing with me a gilded apple,
    a silver-haired candle,
    a flamingo flown here from Egypt,
To travel into fairy tales,
Courting the princess of Candy Kindgom.

But
Mom said:
"Now you must work."

O Night of Myths

1.

Night that is
Humid
Giddy

Night in which
Owlets travel
Bats return

Night in which
Lightning saws a dark cloud into two,
As rains, like sawdust,
Fall as if weeping.

Night in which
Will-o'-the-wisp is spinning
Sickgreen saliva

Bleak, not bleak?

2

Winds are blowing
Rains are beating

I visit the outskirt plains in winds and rains

With clotted blood-wounds.
I want to cry
To cry for
The melancholy kneaded and knotted
With earthworms and soil in the daytime.

Where rains fall,
All miry mud.

3

An old man tells a myth.

    Misty night.
There were often a group of horses,
Mountain-felling, sea-pouring,
Resounding across the prairie.

Cocks crowed.
Warriors,
Jingling, jingling,
Torches shaking,
Returned to their outposts,
Their hands holding some heads.

The next day
In the mist-filled wilderness
Were found white bones
Like corals.

4

In the night
A meteorite fell.
A myth-telling old man died,
Like sleeping—

I thought of
His tombstone.

Now
Fighting always begins with night.
If I should die
Before dawn comes
Then, night will be a tombstone . . . . . .

5

Night is a gambler
With countless pearls
And a silver dollar . . . . . .

There is a small river dreaming as it gurgles.
There is an ear of corn glimmering like jewels.
There are insects playing a symphony . . . . . .

This is rich enough.
Let me have some dews.
Saying "I'm drunk. I'm drunk"
I return to sleep.

The next day I get up early
And dissolve myself
Into the battalion of sounds.

6

Night in which
There is proceeding
There is staying
There is retreating after defeat.

Night that is
Pale
Sick
Tottering

There is light
Flowing out from clouds' doorsill, like milk,

Or, shall we say, night's tears.

When the light is turned off,
When the candle is extinguished,

When cocks crow,
When I sing,

I kneel down
Toward the East
And bid farewell to night.

O Life, fresh life
That climbs out of dream's valley
That is steamed out of night,
Greetings to you,

Greetings!
To You!
To everybody!

I will ride a horse
Neigh
Neigh
Neighing
Toward the jungle
For fresher air.

The Poets' Names in Pinyin and Wade-Giles Systems as well as Chinese

PINYIN	WADE-GILES	Chinese
Feng Zhi	Feng Chih	冯至
Dai Wangshu	Tai Wang-shu	戴望舒
Ai Qing	Ai Ch'ing	艾青
Bian Zhilin	Pien Chih-lin	卞之琳
He Qifang	Ho Ch'i-fang	何其芳
Cao Baohua	Ts'ao Pao-hua	曹葆华
Zhang Kejia	Tsang K'o-chia	臧克家
Xin Di	Hsin Ti	辛笛
Wu Xinghua	Wu Hsing-hua	吴兴华
Mu Dan	Mu Tan	穆旦
Du Yunxie	Tu Yun-Hsieh	杜运燮
Zheng Min	Cheng Min	郑敏
Chen Jingrong	Ch'en Ching-jung	陈敬容
Hang Yuehe	Hang Yueh-he	杭约赫
Tang Qi	T'ang Ch'i	唐祈
Tang Shi	T'ang Shih	唐湜
Yuan Kejia	Yuan K'o-chia	袁可嘉
Lu Yuan	Lu Yuan	绿原

About the Poets

Feng Zhi (1905–)

After graduation from Beijing University, Feng went to Heidelberg University where he majored in German Literature with special emphasis on Rilke. Feng began his career as a poet very early and was active in two poetry societies which he founded with his friends: *Qiancao* (*Low Grass*, 1924), and *Chen-zhong* (*Weighty Bell*, 1925). Two volumes of poems came out of this period: *Yesterday's Songs* (1929), and *Trip to the North and Others* (1929); it was his *Sonnets* (1942) that gained him recognition as a major poet.

Feng is a master of attention to detail and the recognition of the solemn existences of ordinary things. On this level, he is very much like his mentor Rilke, in particular, the Rilke of "The Panther", but unlike Rilke, his trancelike attentiveness never leads to the kind of metaphysical unrest one would find in the Rilke of "Sonnets to Orpheus" and "Duino Elegies". Feng is always grounded in the real.

Dai Wangshu (1905–1950)

Educated in Shanghai, Paris and Madrid, Dai was one of the first poets in the early thirties to synthesize the classical Chinese legacy, the *ci* form, with that of the French symbolists among whom he has found some parallels and affinities. Bian Zhilin, in a preface to Dai's collection of poems written thirty years after Dai's death, outlines three stages of his poetry. The first stage is the combination of the Chinese *ci* and Verlaine. Here, according to Bian, there are still residues of the sentimentalism of the Crescent poets of the 1920s. The second stage is the breaking away from poetic diction to the use of distinctively ordinary speech with control of cadence, a musically conditioned flow prepared by the first stage. "My memory" represents this particular change. The third stage comes with the poem "With my Maimed Palm" in which the poet returns to the stark realities of war-torn China.

Poetry: *My Memory* (1929); *Wangshu Poems* (1932); *Drafts of Wangshu Poems* (1937); *Years of Disasters* (1948).

Dai is also a translator of Baudelaire and Lorca.

Ai Qing (1910–)

That Ai Qing, the son of a landlord, educated in Paris as a painter who enjoyed Baudelaire, Rimbaud and Apollinaire, should turn his back on both his landlord class and his symbolist heritage to write and fight exclusively for the unfavored classes, the poverty-stricken peasants of Northern China, risking imprisonment and execution— he was thrown into jail many times by the ruling Nationalists—shows most sharply the imminence and the sacredness of the call of revolution at that juncture of history in China.

But unlike many of the action-oriented poets of his time whose poetry often ended up as a series of sloganistic shouts, Ai Qing was able to use his Symbolist techniques and integrate them in dramatic and cinematically distinctive powerful images into his engaged projects. In many ways, he is like Neruda, whom he later met, when both became admirers of one another. Like Neruda, but not influenced by him, as some people have anachronistically claimed, both came, in part, from the Symbolist tradition and both were driven by the dire condition of their people to turn their attention to their destinies and meditate on their ancient lands with a moving love and commitment. Unlike Neruda, however, Ai Qing never attempted to transcend the *here* and the *now*. His is never the metaphysical unrest that plagues all the Symbolist poets, including Neruda, but down-to-earth agonies and tragedies.

Bian Zhilin (1910–)

Bian Zhilin has been penalized, unjustly I think, by literary historians for being "difficult". The difficulty will evaporate if one is willing to dissociate oneself from the one-dimensional, goal-directed habits of reading, and allow oneself an openness to various interpretive approaches simultaneously. As I have suggested in my Introduction, the structural interplay Bian maintains between the native (in Bian's case, Daoist) poetic horizon which admits one form of multidimensionality and indeterminancy and the Symbolist poetic world which admits another form of multidimensionality and indeterminancy, and the tension this fused horizon has with the one-dimensional scientific syllogistic progression the new Chinese poetry has adopted from the logical West, have given us one of the richest kinds of poetry in contemporary China.

Bian is versatile. More that half of his poetic output is conversational in that he capitalizes on the modulation of the voice, punctuated by a subtle manipulation of pauses in rhythmic structure. This style he inherited from Xu Zhimo and Wen Yiduo of the Crescent Society. Although most of this poetry is not ambiguous at all; it is also true that poems like "Composition of Distances", "White Shell" and " Round Jewel-Box" generated the most heated dynamic discussions and debates of the 1930s. Bian is also famous for his translations of Symbolist writings, Shakespeare, Brecht and Auden.

Poetry: Three *Autumns: Poems* (1933.); *Fish Eyes* (1935); *Han Garden* (1936), with He Qifang and Li Guangtien ; *Ten Years of Poetry*, (1940).

He Qifang

Although He Qifang openly denounced "clouds, moons and stars" in a manifesto poem, "Clouds" (1937), he will probably be remembered, ironically, for his poems on "clouds, moons and stars." He Qifang, like Bian, is quite typical of modern Chinese intellectuals whose education ranged widely from classical Chinese literature to almost anything Western that they could lay their hands on. Before the age of fifteen, He Qifang has already read his Li Bai, Du Fu, Bai Juyi, Han Yu, Su Shi, Lu You and almost all the classical Chinese novels. When he entered Beijing University, he was immediately converted to new Chinese literature and began to avidly read Western authors like Turgenev, Chekov, Maupassant, Shakespeare, etc. His poetry published before 1937 is full of resonance, both in theme and in rhythm, with the traditional *ci* poems. Indeed, gaudy, elaborate, baroque, dreamlike, sentimental, melancholy are some of the epithets often used to describe him, but in the midst of all these, one also feels a mellowness, a tenderness plus a good-natured warmth of the old world beautifully rehearsed.

Poetry: *Han Garden* (1936), with Bian Zhilin and Li Guangtien; *Conscious Crafting* (1938); *Night Songs* (1934); *Night Songs and Day Songs* (1952)

Cao Baohua (1906–1978)

Cao began as a Crescent poet, rigid in form and sentimental in expression, but with the publication of his *Fugitive Stanzas* or *Untitled* in 1937, he focused on a unique sense of the uneasiness of life. The poems are full of metaphysical and meditative flights into the Wheel of Life and Death in which we find man doomed to become ashes in the cycle of kalpa. Images of bleakness and ghostliness abound.

More influential and perhaps better remembered is his compilation and translation of modern poetic theories—Valery, Eliot, I.A.Richards etc., a book widely read by the poets of the 1940s. Cao is also a famous translator of Shakespeare.

Zhang Kejia (1910–)

Zhang, often mentioned as the best representative of peasant poets, began as a follower of Wen Yiduo who was particularly concerned with the architecture of a poem. Zhang once compared writing to a volcano about to erupt, the most pregnant moment before explosion and he was extremely conscious of the making of the word, the line and the drive of the poem. "What we want from the poets is not the beauty of external form, but the inner dynamic." This artistic concern sets him off from other didactic, sloganistic poets. Indeed, Zhang and Ai Qing were the two action-oriented poets who could *also* appreciate the artistic poets, and had, on various occacions, given the latter spiritual support.

Poetry: *Brand* (1933); *The Black Hand of Sin* (1934); *Self Portrait* (1936); *Canal* (1936); *Join the Army* (1938); *The Song of Earth* (1943); *The Zero of Life* (1947).

Xin Di, or Wang Xindi (1912–)

Xin Di was graduated from Qinghua University in 1935 with a BA in English. In 1936, a year before Japan's all-out invasion of China, he went to England and did research in Edinburgh University and met T. S. Eliot, Spender, Lewis, and Muir. His stay in England and travels in Europe inspired some of his finest lyrics. Xin Di is perhaps the best poet who reinscribes the classical Chinese poetic world in *baihua*. His reinscription lies not just in imagery, which I briefly discussed in the Introduction, but also in the inner twists and turns of emotion approximated by extended sounds and variable pauses in the lines and a sort of inner dialogue through echoes and correspondences. His lyrics demand that we read them aloud over and over again so that we can roam around, affirm, hesitate, reaffirm . . . between the gaps of images and sounds. According to Xin Di, his mentors had been *ci* poems as appropriated by Dai Wangshu, the "Untitled" poems of Li Shangyin of the late Tang period and the poems of Kong Dingan of the Qing Dynasty.

He returned to China in 1939 and taught at Jinan and Guanghua Universities before taking up a position in a bank. He was on the editorial board of one of the most important poetry journals of his time, *Zhongguo Xinshi* (*New Chinese Poetry*) and the *American Literature Series*. He practically stopped writing poetry during the Mao Era, since he, like most of the intellectuals and poets, was sent to labor camps where he could do nothing but compose classical Chinese poetry privately. After the fall of the Gang of Four, he was rehabilitated and is now a committee member of the Chinese Writers' Association in Shanghai, and consultant to many literary organizations. His major works include *Pearls and Shells* (1935), *Palms* (1948), and a collection of notes on literature (1948). He reemerged as a major voice, together with eight leading poets of his time, in an anthology entitled *Nine Leaves Anthology* (1981).

Wu Xinghua (1921–1966)

Legend has it that Wu could play a game of chess and write poetry at the same time. As a poet, he is obsessively concerned with form, determined to make sure that the *baihua* (plain speech) can comfortably accommodate various formal structures. Therefore, almost all his poems confront the challenge of formal constructions: equal numbers of metrical pauses for each line, complex rhyming schemes, his experimenting with classical Chinese forms such as the *jueju* (four-line "curtailed poems"), and subtle echoes in metrical progression. Indeed, his last work, a translation of Dante's *Divine Comedy*, which was unfortunately destroyed by the Red Guards who caused his death, follows closely the original complex rhyming scheme of *terza rima*. Deeply believing in the possibility of giving classical Chinese a new form, he attempts a kind of dramatic narrative by rewriting famous historical events. "The Woman Who Played the *Pipa*," for example , is meant, to echo Bai Juyi's (772–846) "Song of the Pipa," but it is written in a kind of blank verse with a metrical approximation of the iambic pentameter of the West.

Mu Dan (1918–1977)

Mu's poetry is *weighty* and *dynamic*. These two epithets are not chosen arbitrarily. *Weightiness* without being *dynamic* is clumsy; *dynamic* without *weightiness* can be all surface. *Weightiness* here means "weightiness in content," in particular, the tragic burden of China in the 1940s, "weightiness in thought", the inward groping for space, and "weightiness in form matching content": depth, scope and density, i.e., philosophical quest and questioning, leap of imagination, and condensation (no superfluous word), as well as multi-leveled radiation of meanings. *Dynamic* means blooded activity, energized flow of images and sounds in the midst of plurisignifications. Mu Dan's poetry is not easy, but patience in reading pays off. The more one reads, the deeper and wider one's view becomes.

Educated at Southwest Associated University in Kunming during the War of Resistance against the Japanese and at Chicago University where he received an MA in English, Mu Dan is versatile, and one of the strongest poets in the Nine Leaves. Aside from three volumes of poetry: *Explorer*, (1945); *Flag*, (1948) and *Poems of Mu Dan* (1947), he is also a translator, with excellent style equivalents, of Pushkin, O'Neil, Shelley, Keats, Byron and Blake.

Du Yunxie (1918–)

Du was born in Malaysia, but came back to China to study. He was graduated from the English Department of the Southwest Associated University in Kunming. During the War of Resistance against the Japanese, he worked as an interpreter in India and Burma, where he composed some of his unique poetry about his war experiences.

Du's poems exhibit a quiet, controlled and unhurried lyricism with a lightly trembling flow of undercurrents of feelings that threaten to break through their calm surface. He achieves this with arresting images and by following attentively the exact curves of the objects and events that silently affect and transform a vigilant consciousness.

Poetry: *Forty Poems* (1946). A good representation of his poetry of this period can also be found in the *Nine Leaves Anthology*.

Zheng Min (1920–)

Zheng Min, like many of the Nine Leaves poets, was educated in the Philosophy Department of the Southwest Associated University and later she received an MA in English from Brown University in the U.S. To Zheng Min, poetry is the tip of the tower of culture. Without it, all culture would be at a loss—a soulless mass of activities. To guard against the reification of man, against the exile of the soul, we write poetry.

From 1961 to the present, Zheng has been a professor of English and American literature at North Normal University in Beijing. She has written extensively on drama, poetry and critical theories, and has translated a volume of contemporary American poetry (1987). The poems included in this anthology are taken from her *Poems 1942–47*.

Chen Jingrong (1917–1989)

Chen Jingrong was a distinctive female voice in the forties who started publishing just before Japan's full-scale invasion of China. In 1946, she went to Shanghai and emerged as an important poet and translator. In the capacity of an editor of *Zhongguo Xinshi* (*New Chinese Poetry*), she wrote important commentaries aimed at correcting the overly sloganistic trend of her time.

Poetry: *Symphony* (1947); *Brimming Full* (1948). Chen has translated works of Anderson, Hugo, Pushkin and others.

Hang Yuehe (1917–)

Hang Yuehe is the penname of Cao Xinji. The penname is known as a poet, while Cao is known as an artist, a book designer. Educated at the Ceramic Arts School and Normal College in Kiangsu Province, he briefly became a primary school teacher before he began to edit the literary magazine *Pinghua*. When the Sino-Japanese War broke out, Cao went to Shanxi and entered the University of National Revolution, and, in 1938, he went to Yenan where he studied in the Lu Xun Arts College. In Shanghai in the late 1940s, he started two of the most influential poetry magazines, *Shi Chuangzhao* (*Poetry Creation*), and *Zhongguo Xinshi* (*New Chinese Poetry*), both of which contain some of the most important poems and discourses on poetry of the 1940s.

Poetry: *Plucking Stars* (1945); *Nightmare* (1947); *Burning City* (1948) and a long poem entitled *Resurrected Earth* (1949).

Tang Shi (1920–)

Aside from being a fine lyricist, Tang Shi was also a devoted apologist for the poetry of his contemporaries. In his volume of critical essays *Poetic Sense Measured* (1950), for example, he has written on Feng Zhi, Zheng Min, Xin Di, Mu Dan, Chen Jingrong, Tang Qi, and others, most of whom were later grouped with him as the Nine Leaves Poets.

Tang graduated from the Foreign Languages and Literatures Department of Zhejiang University and he was on the editorial committee of both *Shi Chuangzhao* (*Poetry Creation*) and *Zhongguo Xinshi* (*New Chinese Poetry*). He is familiar with many symbolist and post-symbolist writers, including Valery and Eliot to whom he often refers in his essays. He is also a translator of many important works: Shakespeare, Shelley, Keats, Milton, Rilke, and Eliot ("Burnt Norton").

Poetry: *Tumultuous City* (1947); *The Prairie of Heroes* (1948) and *Songs in Flight* (1950).

Tang Qi (1920–1990)

To quote Tang Qi: "Except for that little bit of naive softness of my youthful days, I have never really sung of anything. When I think of the fact that I can only bring out from these darkened things and events in society a bigger image of emptiness as it is, I become anxious and want more and more to revolt, as I become more and more angry."

A history major from Northwest Associated University, he wrote many lyrics that reflected the life of the Northwest provinces before he turned toward the agonizing reality of metropolitan Shanghai under the shadows of the Concessions. ("Time and Banner", 1948).

Yuan Kejia (1921–)

The youngest of the Nine Leaves, Yuan Kejia was another apologist for the kind of poetry his contemporaries practiced. Like Mu Dan and Du Yunxie, he was also graduated from Southwest Associated University, a wartime university where some of the best minds of the 1930s in China (Feng Zhi, Bian Zhilin, etc.) and examples from the modern tradition in the West (the Symbolists, Rilke, Eliot, Richards, Auden via William Empson, Feng and Bian, their teachers) converged.

In Yuan's view, poetry is the refinement, sublimation and crystalization of life. Poetry cannot be separated from politics, but it should not be dominated by it. He is opposed to sloganistic poetry and political sentimentalism, but he is also opposed to the aesthetic tendency of the academic poets. He advocates the modernization of poetry (essays written between 1947–48, collected in *On the Modernization of New Poetry*, 1988), in which he maintains that, in terms of thought, while poetry should reflect major social issues, the poet should retain a free expressive space . . . and in terms of artistic manipulation, the poet should develop thinking in images and the fusion of the intellect and the intuitive.

A translator of Burns and others, he has put together recently a most comprehensive collection of Western Modernist Writings.

Lu Yuan (1922–)

Lu Yuan began publishing in 1941 and his first book, *Children's Tales* (1942) won him instant acclaim. The assimilated voice and perceptual stance from the world of children have helped him create for us some of the freshest images and narrative turns and have given us a unique passage for the often stark realities trembling behind them.

About the Editor

Wai-lim Yip: Bibliographical Summary

Active as a bi-cultural poet, translator, critic and theorist between Taiwan and America for over 20 years, Professor Wai-lim Yip was born in Kwangtung Province, China, in 1937. He received his BA (1959) and MA (1961) in English in Taiwan where he became a leading modernist poet and theorist and won many literary prizes, including a literary award from the Ministry of Education, a best poetry award from the Association of Chinese Writers, and recognition as one of the Ten Major Modern Chinese Poets. In 1964, he was conferred an MFA by the University of Iowa for a volume of original English poems, and in 1967, he obtained a Ph.D. in Comparative Literature at Princeton University.

Professor Yip's interests are multiple, but his crowning achievement comes from a lifelong commitment to creating and critiquing poetry in a cross-cultural context. As a poet, he attempts to synthesize the heritage of the Chinese poets of the 1940s, the expressive strategies of the West since Symbolism, and those of classical Chinese poetry. As a critic and theorist on East-West comparative poetics, he has provided new pedagogical guidelines to break the monocultural perpetuation of certain critical and theoretical hypotheses as the sole authority on the subject of literature and culture, leading to a truly open dialogue between Chinese and Western Cultures in an inter-illuminating and inter-reflective manner.

Professor Yip has written more than thirty books in two languages. Chief among them are: Poetry: *Fugue, Crossing, Edge of Waking, The Wild Flower Story, The Voice of Blooming, The Legend of a Pine and a Bird, Startled, Travelling, Spring: Travelling, The Ferry that cannot be detained,* and *Thirty Years of Poetry*; Criticism and Theory: *Ezra Pound's Cathay,*

Phenomenon, Experience, Expression, Order's Growth, Critical Essays on Modern Chinese Writers, Classical Chinese Literature in Comparative Perspective, Comparative Poetics, and *Dialogues with Modern, Chinese Painters;* Translations with critical and theoretical introductory essays: *Modern Chinese Poetry, Hiding the Universe: Poems of Wang Wei,* and *Chinese Poetry: Major Modes and Genres;* Translations into Chinese: T. S. Eliot's *Waste Land,* St.-John Perse, Seferis, Guillen, Paz, etc.

Professor Yip has been on the staff of the University of California at San Diego since 1968, and was, for many years, Chairman of Comparative Literature and a member of the Chinese Studies Program, but his influence abroad is as significant and extensive. In 1970 and 1974, as visiting professor in National Taiwan University, he helped to launch the first Ph.D. Program in East-West Comparative Literature in China, and again between 1980–82, he took up the Chair Professorship in the Chinese University of Hong Kong where he became instrumental in setting up an M. Phil. in Comparative Literature, which has directly influenced the Comparative Literature Association in Peking. He has been invited by the Academy of Social Sciences, Peking University, Association of Chinese Writers (Peking) to give several series of lectures on Comparative Literature, Modernism, and Recent Critical Theory in Peking, Shanghai, Harbin, and Guanzhou, including a special session for representative professors from nationwide universities in Shenzhen. A selection of his comparative literary studies entitled *In Search of Common Poetics,* which has become an instant bestseller in China was made by Wen Ru-min of Peking University (1987). At the same time, the ten books on East-West Comparative Literature edited by him (including his own *Comparative Poetics*) published in Taipei have been avidly read by scholars on both sides of the Taiwan Strait. Between 1987 and 1988, Tai-tung Press in Taipei honored Professor Yip by putting out a boxed set of five volumes of his poetry, lyrical prose and comments on modern Chinese painting.

Some Titles in the Series

JAMES J. WILHELM
General Editor

1. Lars Ahlin, *Cinnamoncandy*.
   Translated from Swedish by Hanna Kalter Weiss.

2. *Anthology of Belgian Symbolist Poets*.
   Translated from French by Donald F. Friedman.

3. Ariosto, *Five Cantos*.
   Translated from Italian by Leslie Z. Morgan.

4. Enrique Medina, *Las Tumbas*. Translated from Spanish by David William Foster.

5. Antonio de Castro Alves, *The Major Abolitionist Poems*.
   Translated from Portuguese by Amy A. Peterson.

6. Li Cunbao, *The Wreath at the Foot of the Mountain*.
   Translated from Chinese by Chen Hanming and James O. Belcher.

7. Meïr Goldschmidt, *A Jew*.
   Translated from Danish by Kenneth Ober.

8. Árpád Göncz, *Plays and Other Writings*.
   Translated from Hungarian by Katharina and Christopher Wilson.

9. Ramón Hernández, *Invitation to Die.*
   Translated from Spanish by Marion Freeman.

10. Edvard Hoem, *The Ferry Crossing.*
    Translated from New Norwegian by
    Frankie Denton Shackelford.

11. Henrik Ibsen, "*Catiline*" *and* "*The Burial Mound.*"
    Translated from Dano-Norwegian by Thomas Van Laan.

12. Banabhatta, *Kadambari: A Classical Hindu Story of Magical Transformations.* Translated from Sanskrit by
    Gwendolyn Layne.

13. *Selected Poems of Lina Kostenko.*
    Translated from Ukrainian by Michael Naydan.

14. Baptista Mantuanus, *Adulescentia: The Eclogues of Mantuan.*
    Translated from Latin by Lee Piepho.

15. *The Mourning Songs of Greek Women.*
    Translated from Greek by Konstantinos Lardas.

16. *Ono no Komachi: Poems, Stories, and Noh Plays.*
    Translated from Japanese by Roy E., Nicholas J.,
    and Helen Rebecca Teele.

17. Adam Small, *Kanna, He Is Coming Home.*
    Translated from Afrikaans by Carrol Lasker.

18. Federigo Tozzi, *Ghisola.*
    Translated from Italian by Charles Klopp.

19. *The Burden of Sufferance: Women Poets in Russia.*
    Translated from Russian by Albert Cook and Pamela Perkins.

20. Chantal Chawaf, *Mother Love, Mother Earth.*
    Translated from French by Monique Nagem.

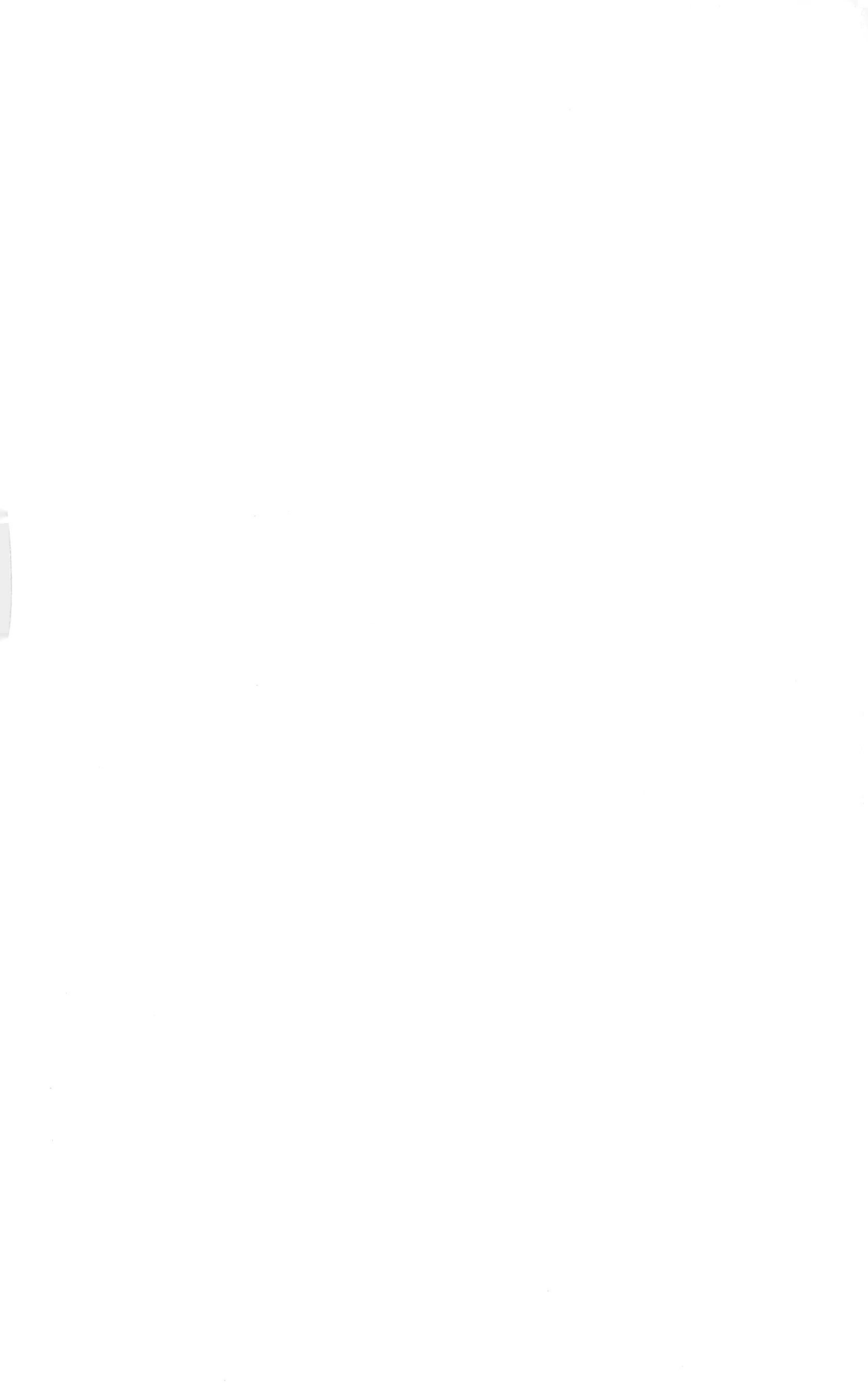